FOCUS ON INERTIA

Hands-On STEM

by Joanne Mattern

FOCUS READERS

www.focusreaders.com

Focus Readers is distributed by North Star Editions:
sales@northstareditions.com | 888-417-0195

Produced for Focus Readers by Red Line Editorial.

Content Consultant: Bruce Bolon, Associate Professor of Physics, Hamline University

Photographs ©: Kuznetcov_Konstantin/Shutterstock Images, cover, 1; Nor Gal/Shutterstock Images, 4–5; MsSponge/iStockphoto, 7; duncan1890/iStockphoto, 8–9; ttsz/iStockphoto, 11; sgtphoto/iStockphoto, 13; monkeybusinessimages/iStockphoto, 15; shironosov/iStockphoto, 17; FatCamera/iStockphoto, 18–19; IPGGutenbergUKLtd/iStockphoto, 21; JSC/NASA, 23; travelview/Shutterstock Images, 25, 29; Red Line Editorial, 27

ISBN
978-1-63517-283-6 (hardcover)
978-1-63517-348-2 (paperback)
978-1-63517-478-6 (ebook pdf)
978-1-63517-413-7 (hosted ebook)

Library of Congress Control Number: 2017935127

Printed in the United States of America
Mankato, MN
June, 2017

About the Author

Joanne Mattern is the author of many nonfiction books for children. Her favorite subjects include science, history, and biography. She hopes to make nonfiction fun for young readers. Joanne lives in New York with her husband, four children, and several pets.

TABLE OF CONTENTS

CHAPTER 1

Stop and Go 5

CHAPTER 2

What Is Inertia? 9

CHAPTER 3

Inertia in Everyday Life 19

SCIENCE IN ACTION!

Inertia with Money 26

Focus on Inertia • 28

Glossary • 30

To Learn More • 31

Index • 32

STOP AND GO

Hannah's dad is driving her to school. Suddenly, a dog darts in front of the car. Hannah's dad slams on the brakes. The car comes to a fast stop. But Hannah's body keeps moving forward.

A car comes to a sudden stop when the brakes are pressed hard.

Fortunately, Hannah is wearing her seat belt. The seat belt helps stop her motion as the car slows down. Without the seat belt, Hannah would keep moving forward. That's because all objects tend to keep doing what they are already doing. This is called inertia.

A moving object tends to keep moving. Its speed and direction will not change unless a net **force** acts on the object. A net force is the

> **Wearing a seat belt is important when riding in cars.**

total effect of all forces acting on the object.

CHAPTER 2

WHAT IS INERTIA?

Long ago, people did not understand why objects behaved the way they did. But in the late 1600s, Isaac Newton changed people's understanding. He wrote about how forces act on objects.

Isaac Newton lived from 1643 to 1727.

Newton described three laws of motion. His first law explains inertia. This law says objects **resist** changes in motion.

For example, when an object is not moving, it tends to stay at rest. The object will not move unless a net force acts on it. Similarly, when an object is moving, it tends to keep the same speed in the same direction. The speed and direction will not change unless a net force acts on the object.

INERTIA IN ACTION

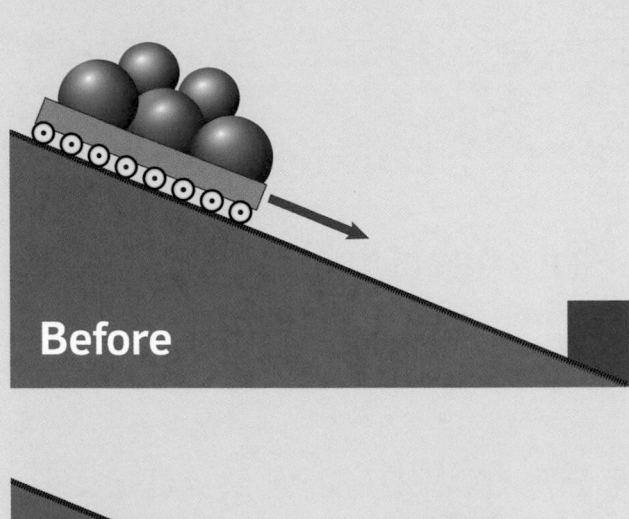

Before

After

 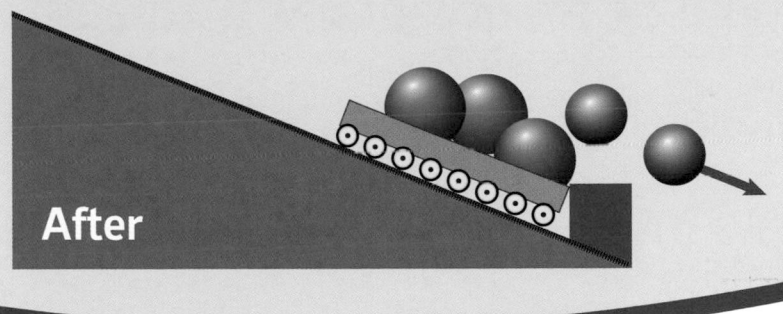

A force causes the cart to stop. Two of the balls stay in motion because a force did not act on them.

Some motion happens in a straight line. For this type of motion, the object's **mass** is a measurement of its inertia.

For instance, suppose an object has a large mass. That means the object has a lot of inertia. It is difficult to change the object's motion. Now suppose an object has a small mass. That means the object has less inertia. It is easier to change the object's motion.

Not all motion happens in a straight line. Motion can also happen in a circle. For example, think of a spinning wheel. This is known as **rotational** motion.

A train has a large amount of mass, so it has a lot of inertia.

For rotation, a different type of inertia is involved. It is known as the moment of inertia.

Some objects have a large moment of inertia. With these objects, it is hard to change their rotational motion. Other objects have a small moment of inertia. With these objects, it is easier to change their rotational motion.

An object's mass affects the moment of inertia. How the mass is spread out matters, too. For

> **Bicycle wheels have rotational motion.**

instance, think about a group

of kids on a merry-go-round.

Suppose the kids are near the edge. The merry-go-round is hard to turn. Now suppose the kids are near the center. The merry-go-round is easier to turn. The moment of inertia is larger when the kids are near the edge. It is smaller when they are near the center. A larger moment of inertia means it is harder to change the merry-go-round's rotational motion.

 The moment of inertia is affected by how the people are spread out.

CHAPTER 3

INERTIA IN EVERYDAY LIFE

Inertia plays an important role in our everyday lives. It affects us every time we touch objects. Suppose you kick a ball that is at rest. The ball's inertia affects how fast it will go after the kick.

 **Inertia is an important part of sports.**

The larger the inertia, the slower the ball will go. The inertia of your foot matters, too. If you miss the ball, your foot keeps going.

Imagine trying to push a box across a slippery floor. A slippery floor does not have much **friction**. The box has mass, though. That means it has inertia. The box will remain at rest unless there is a net force. The larger the mass, the harder it is to change the box's motion. A heavy box will not speed

The heavier an object is, the larger the force needed to get the same change in motion.

up as easily as a light box. This is

because of inertia.

Gravity is a force we deal with every day. In space, gravity's effect on an object is very small compared to when the object is on Earth. But the ideas of inertia still apply in space.

Think about an astronaut holding a tool in space. If she lets go, her tool will seem to stay where it was. The gravitational force on the tool is very small. The tool was not moving before it was released. Because of its inertia, it will barely

In space, the astronaut's book does not fall to the floor.

move after it is released. Things are different on Earth. The tool would fall to the ground. That's because there is a net force on the tool due to gravity.

You can also think of inertia as a measurement of an object's **stability**. If an object has a lot of inertia, it is harder to change what the object is doing.

For example, think of a large truck speeding down the highway. It is hard to change the truck's motion. Now think of a small car on the highway. It is easier to change the car's motion. That's because the car has less inertia.

 **Compared to a car, it is easy to change a skateboard's motion.**

INERTIA WITH MONEY

What will happen when you pull a smooth piece of paper out from under a stack of coins? Do this experiment to find out.

Step 1: Put a dollar bill on the table. If you do not have a dollar bill, use a similar-sized piece of paper.

Step 2: Put a stack of 10 to 15 coins on one end of the dollar bill. If you do not have coins, use a stack of similar-sized flat objects.

Step 3: Quickly pull away the dollar bill. Did the coins fall?

The coins will not move much if you pull the paper quickly.

How does the idea of inertia relate to this experiment? What might happen if you pulled the dollar bill slowly? Would the result be different? Why?

FOCUS ON
INERTIA

Write your answers on a separate piece of paper.

1. Write a sentence that explains the main idea of Chapter 2.

2. Would you want to live in space? Why or why not?

3. What happens to a moving object if no net forces act on it?

    A. The object keeps the same speed in the same direction.

    B. The object keeps the same speed, but it moves in a different direction.

    C. The object changes speed but keeps moving in the same direction.

4. Which of these three objects has the most inertia?

    A. a golf ball

    B. a tennis ball

    C. a bowling ball

5. What does **darts** mean in this book?

*Suddenly, a dog **darts** in front of the car. Hannah's dad slams on the brakes.*

    A. moves slowly

    B. moves quickly

    C. moves quietly

6. What does **role** mean in this book?

*Inertia plays an important **role** in our everyday lives. It affects us every time we touch objects.*

    A. a time of day

    B. a way to move

    C. a part in a process

Answer key on page 32.

GLOSSARY

force
A push or pull that one object has on another.

friction
The roughness between two surfaces that are in contact with each other.

gravity
The force one object has on another due to the mass of each object and how far apart they are.

mass
The amount of matter in an object.

resist
To try to keep something from happening.

rotational
Having to do with circular movements.

stability
How difficult it is to change something.

TO LEARN MORE

BOOKS

Mooney, Carla. *Isaac Newton: Genius Mathematician and Physicist*. Minneapolis: Abdo Publishing, 2015.

Pascal, Janet. *Who Was Isaac Newton?* New York: Grosset & Dunlap, 2014.

Steele, Philip. *Isaac Newton: The Scientist Who Changed Everything*. Washington, DC: National Geographic Children's Books, 2013.

NOTE TO EDUCATORS

Visit **www.focusreaders.com** to find lesson plans, activities, links, and other resources related to this title.

INDEX

D

direction, 6, 10

F

friction, 20

G

gravity, 22–23

M

mass, 11–12, 14, 20
moment of inertia, 14, 16
motion, 6, 10–12, 14, 16,
    20, 24

N

net force, 6, 10, 20, 23
Newton, Isaac, 9–10

R

rest, 10, 19–20
rotational motion,
    12–14, 16

S

space, 22
speed, 6, 10, 20, 24
stability, 24

Answer Key: 1. Answers will vary; **2.** Answers will vary; **3.** A; **4.** C; **5.** B; **6.** C

OPPORTUNITIES IN
PSYCHIATRY

Fenton Keyes

Vocational Guidance Manuals
A Division of Data Courier, Inc.
Louisville, Kentucky

Copyright © 1977
Vocational Guidance Manuals
A Division of
Data Courier, Inc.
620 South Fifth Street
Louisville, Kentucky 40202

Publisher—Loene Trubkin
Editor—Christine Maddox
Assistant Editor—Gary Barker
Photo Editor—Donna Lawrence
Production Manager—Carmen Chetti
Production Supervisor—Sylvia Ward
Production—Tammy Crumpton
Administrative Services—Cynthia Pierce

Manufactured in the
United States of America

Library of Congress Catalog Card Number 76—42885

ISBN Number   0-89022-230-4 (Hardcover)
               0-89022-231-2 (Paperbound)

Cover photograph by Charlie Westerman

ABOUT THE AUTHOR

Dr. Fenton Keyes writes and consults in the areas of health, social welfare, educational administration, and urban problems. His last three books were career guides to three socially curative fields: mental health, social work, and allied health.

Born and reared in New York and Connecticut, Dr. Keyes received his baccalaureate and doctoral degrees in sociology from Yale University. After working on the faculty of Colgate University, he served during World War II in civilian stateside assignments with Military Intelligence and command assignments with American forces in the China-Burma-India Theater. He was twice decorated with the Bronze Star.

A variety of academic positions followed his military career: Vice President, Skidmore College; Dean of the Faculty and Director of Graduate Studies, Texas Woman's University; and President, Coker College. After eight years in the latter assignment, the attractions of full-time research took him to the Franklin Institute in Philadelphia, where, as Manager of the Behaviorial & Social Sciences Laboratory, he applied systems science and modern evaluation techniques to educational, ecological, and management problems.

Dr. Keyes continues his career in the health field by writing, consulting, and conducting studies such as those recently completed for Thomas Jefferson University and the Council for Higher Education of Newark, New Jersey.

For my children's grandparents

George Evertson Dix
Janet Dortch Dix
Elsie Fenton Keyes
Harold Brown Keyes

IN MEMORIAM

FOREWORD

Presumably, your interest in being helpful, your desire to provide much needed care to others, has led you to this book. The career of psychiatry has rich rewards in that regard, as well as in others. At the same time, there appears to be inherent in it an element of mystery. The challenge of psychiatry is hard to define. It offers its participants the ability and the opportunity to be of great help to the mentally ill and their families—individuals who often need assistance in the most poignant way. More so than in many other specialties, there is the likelihood, probably the certainty, of being able to participate in dramatic breakthroughs in the practice of psychiatry during your lifetime. By any standard, dealing as it does with human beings, psychiatry is more worthwhile and meaningful than many other less dynamic occupations.

Despite the fact that the profession is receptive to the often impatient and critical views of its younger members, psychiatry's evolvement from its conservatism of the past often has been tempered and slowed by the vested interests of some of its senior members.

In view of psychiatry's past failures to involve women and members of minority groups, the profession is making positive and strenuous efforts to recruit them now. Psychiatry is wide open to all individuals whose skill and personal finesse qualify them.

In coming years, the psychiatry profession will continue to grow in size and in terms of public acceptance and esteem. There is a strong likelihood that there will be a significant number of job opportunities throughout the decade of the 1980s and beyond.

By contemporary standards, the economic rewards of psychiatry rank among the top levels. Psychologically and intellectually, the specialty offers endless rewards for those who will let themselves enjoy the "fringe benefits." Socially, there are advantages in connection with associates, patients, and the community doors that swing open to a psychiatrist—all very valuable assets in themselves.

Psychiatry is the very opposite of a dead-end road. It is wide open for the psychiatrist's own growth and development. There are chances to move into a completely different occupation on a full-time basis or to become involved in something new as an avocation, while psychiatry remains the primary area of concentration. If there is one disadvantage which should be mentioned, it would be the fact that the psychiatrist must wrestle with the problem of how best to allocate his time and energies amongst a multitude of fascinating activities over a long and continually stimulating career.

Pronouns appearing in this book are used for reasons of clarity and succinctness. They are not intended to imply exclusion of males or females.

TABLE OF CONTENTS

About The Author iii

Dedication iv

Foreword v

1. The Scope and History of Psychiatry 11

2. What is Mental Illness and
   How Does a Psychiatrist Treat It? 21
   Types of mental illness. Treatment of mental illness.

3. What is a Psychiatrist? 31
   The psychiatrist as a human being. The psychiatrist as
   a professional. The psychiatrist as a citizen. Allied
   specialists.

4. Education for a Psychiatry Career 49
   High school. College. Medical school. Foreign medical
   schools. Large vs. small medical schools. Internship
   and residency. Residency. Financing college and
   medical school. A school budget. Financial aid.

5. Getting Started 77

6. Employment and Salaries
   of Psychiatrists 93
   Type of work. Geographic distribution. Places of
   work. Urban versus rural work. Special community

work. Outlook for the future. Salaries. Salaries of residents.

7. **Professional Accreditation** 105

Licensing. Certification. Professional organizations. The American Psychiatric Association. The American Board of Psychiatry and Neurology. Ethics and the psychiatrist.

8. **Minority Groups and Women in Psychiatry** 111

Minority groups. Special programs. Financial aid. Women.

9. **The Future of Psychiatry** 123

Appendix A—Recommended Reading 131

Appendix B—U.S. Medical Schools 136

Index 142

CHAPTER 1

THE SCOPE AND HISTORY OF PSYCHIATRY

In the broadest sense, psychiatry is that branch of medical science which deals with the mentally ill; that is, their care, cure, study, and need for greater public understanding and better protection under our laws. For our purposes, the mentally ill are those whose abnormality, the extent—small or great—of their difference from the cultural norm, creates problems both for themselves and for others.

In all of contemporary psychiatry, there is a continuum approach to mental illness, namely, that all of us are distributed along a mental health-illness progression. The sequence has one end solidly based in patently normal, well-adjusted behavior; the other end, at the diametrically different extreme, is characterized by complete inability to live, work, and play in today's society. Not only are all of us distributed along this spectrum of behavior but our exact location varies from time to time, often minute to minute.

If we are honest with ourselves, all of us will admit to having mood swings, with times when we feel happy, elated, or in an "all's right with the world" state of mind, as opposed to periods when we feel depressed, discouraged, and when the day appears to be one blunder, misfortune, and rejection after another. Of course, when we act within the general parameters of normality, no problem exists. On the other hand, the individual needing help is characterized by behavior which is obviously not in harmony with the social norm. An example? Society accepts and may even praise and esteem the person who defends his house and family against invaders; it reacts with revulsion, indignation, and harsh punishment when a person kills senselessly, or even threatens or menaces a public figure. Senseless murder or assassination are two of the many possible extreme or pronounced examples of maladaptive behavior.

From time to time, all of us engage in what might be called some form of mental therapy. We compliment or praise a friend who seems downcast; we "kid" an associate, hoping in this way to nudge him into accepting or rationalizing an unpleasant assignment, rejection, or demotion. Sensitive or discerning people can often identify the mood of another family member and so act as to make him less tense or tired and more self-sufficient.

However, when confronted by a severely disturbed person, our usual reaction is one of helplessness or even terror, particularly when the behavior falls into one of the following categories: 1) distress, as manifested by such symptoms as worry and agitation, dysphoria (disorder of mood), or a generalized feeling of ill-being, especially abnormal anxiety, discontent, physical discomfort, etc.; 2) disorganization, as reflected in gross confusion, flight of ideas, hallucinations, delusions, and psychomotor retardation; and 3) disruptive acts that are either totally inappropriate, or involve violence or some criminal conduct.

We react to abnormal behavior with a certain degree of terror because of the instinctive identification we make with this disturbed human being—because he or she is "one of us," is so much like us but is, somehow, out of control. We are frightened because a person like ourselves is displaying abnormal behavior, and we have no way of predicting what will happen next. Inasmuch as we see responses which are inconsistent with our expectations, which are not the usual behavioral adaptations of most people, we recoil from them. Psychiatrists must react differently. They must diagnose the condition that prevents an individual's effective functioning and determine what treatment is needed.

Perhaps the best way to explain how the psychiatric profession tries to care for, cure, and study those who are mentally ill is to cite the goals set forth by the National Institute of Mental Health:

> "To develop fuller knowledge of the causes of mental illness, to provide resources for treating mentally and emotionally troubled persons within their own communities, to enlarge the reservoirs of mental health manpower, and to learn more about how afflictions of the mind can be prevented."

This strategy is reflected in the psychiatrist's major areas of concern, which include the following:

Aging
Alcoholism
Behavior problems
Biochemistry in the treatment of mental illness
Community mental health
Crime and juvenile delinquency
Depression
Family and marital problems
Mass violence
Memory
Mental health of children
Mental hospital improvement
Metropolitan problems
Narcotics and drug abuse
Neurophysiology/neurobiology
Personality disorders
Poverty and mental health
Psychopharmacology
Public education about mental health

Schizophrenia
School mental health
Suicide prevention

To this could be added the psychiatrist's interest in every aspect of human life that appears to affect or be involved with individual and group mental illness or its identification and researching.

The most significant emphases which emerge are the concern with prevention; the hope for future breakthroughs in the areas of treatment and cure by prescribing the appropriate kinds of drugs, chemicals, vitamins, and foods; the recognition that much mental illness and general unhappiness have little or nothing to do with an individual's strengths or weaknesses since they result from destructive environments—a substandard home, family, or neighborhood; identification of the nervous system as a likely source of much mental illness, the hope that, with education and acceptance of community obligation, a great deal of mental illness prevention and cure/care can be handled near home, resulting in an accelerated return of patients to their families, neighborhoods, and jobs.

Early diagnosis and immediate treatment come second only to prevention—the first priority. On balance, this is a heartening analysis of the problem. You can see that, increasingly, mental illness will be approached from the standpoint of both its physical and psychological roots. In order that this approach be effective, the cooperative effort of the following specialists is essential: psychiatrists, neurologists, nurses, pharmacists, psycho-biologists, analytical psychologists, biosocial psychologists, geneticists, anatomists, and sociologists.

A BRIEF HISTORY

The excitement and challenge of contemporary psychiatry are comparatively recent developments. Today's remarkably effective and pervasive rehabilitation programs for our mentally ill are largely post-World War II creations which, even today, still lack complete public understanding and legislative support.

On the other hand, it is a serious mistake to suppose that mental illness and social reaction to it are peculiar to modern life. On the contrary, some of the earliest historical records reflect not only the presence but also the careful observation of the mentally ill. These descriptions have been found on the walls of caves, on such early papyruses as the Ebers Papyrus of 1550 B.C., and in some primitive art works. Additionally, we have found the skeletons of early man whose skulls had been opened by skillful bone surgery. Apparently, primitive man felt that the source of mental ailment lay in the brain; thus, surgeons attempted either to remove the trouble or permit it to escape. The Ebers Papyrus said, "His mind raves through something entering from above." Presumably, this statement was a diagnosis that a spirit had entered the mind of a relative or neighbor and caused unusual behavior.

But early Greek scholars and their pupils must be given credit for a rational, analytical approach to mental disturbances. In the third century B.C., Hippocrates, who is considered the father of medicine, taught that all mental disorders had causes which were completely unconnected with "magic" or "demons." As natural incidents, he said, they should be treated as unrelated to the supernatural. Although some of his ideas were only partly correct, he also observed a connection between mental illness on the one hand and brain pathology, brain injuries, and heredity on the other. Somewhat later, Plato, enlarging on the Hippocratic teachings, condemned those who treated the mentally ill as criminals. Because they were not responsible for their acts, he said, they should be given humane care within the community. In turn, Aristotle, a student of Plato, emphasized the organic nature of much mental illness.

Throughout the centuries which followed, the views of the Greeks were much discussed but were put into practice only

Benjamin Rush (1745-1813), called "the father of American Psychiatry," wrote the first American text on psychiatry.

occasionally. It was not until the Age of Enlightenment that the rationalization of mental disease in religious terms, cruel treatment measures, and brutal imprisonment fell into disrepute.

In the nineteenth century, improved treatment of the mentally handicapped began to emerge in the United States, largely as a result of reformers' success in freeing certain categories of social outcasts from the almshouses, prisons, jails, kennels, and cages where they had been confined. Increased concern for and attention to the mentally ill and deprived, their needs and problems, came gradually. A very few of the older and richer sections of the country made a beginning at treating them more humanely, for example, by boarding them with private families at public expense. There was a scattering of charitable local and state programs like "The Cooperative Society of Visitors Among the Poor" in Boston. The work of Benjamin Franklin and Benjamin Rush, discussed below, was particularly influential.

But attitudes varied tremendously from person to person and from community to community. And with traditional American practicality, the citizens, as taxpayers, put first things first. Top priority was given to subduing the continent, clearing the land, and building schools and churches. The establishment of hospitals had to wait. It is regrettable, but in the early years of this nation's history, unless society's welfare was obviously involved, the most common response to the mentally disabled was to thrust them out of sight and mind. Rarely were rehabilitation benefits or programs allowed to interfere with manpower needs, and there were few rich families and even fewer affluent communities which could afford to finance treatment facilities. There was a long trail to follow before there would be general agreement that our society, however democratic or humanistic, would recognize the mentally ill as worthy of public welfare.

A dramatic change occured in 1756, when that multi-talented American genius, Benjamin Franklin, campaigning for proper care of the mentally ill, was instrumental in opening Pennsylvania Hospital in Philadelphia to the mentally ill. He and Benjamin Rush, the so-called "father of American psychiatry," were determined that the mentally ill would be treated, first as patients and second as individuals, with a right to kindness and human dignity.

But the foundations for today's essentially scientific treatment and cures were not established prior to the insights and teachings of Sigmund Freud. He gave the world a body of theory which explained—or seemed to explain—mental aberrations. By studying unconscious processes of the human personality, Freud and his followers showed us the way to the development of a scientific approach to the study of human behavior. They made us aware now that it was not "devils," punishment for sins, or perversity but, rather, unconscious determinants which usually caused mental illness. These motives, hidden in the unconscious, could be revealed, studied, treated, and, in most cases, explained to patients and their families.

The work of Dorothea Lynde Dix, Clifford Beers, and other reformers paved the way for the ultimate general acceptance of the findings of both United States and European psychiatrists and neurologists. This reception was made possible by the realization that, as with other aspects of medical science, it was essential to adopt and move ahead with new techniques and treatment as they developed. Tragically, however, because delay has always characterized both the development of mental health concepts and their general acceptance, it was not until the 1940s that significant positive steps were actually taken. Gradually, harsh treatment of patients in institutions for the mentally ill was eliminated and therapeutic techniques improved. At the time of World War II, the public became acutely aware of the need to adopt new methods for the treatment and prevention of mental breakdowns. Far more than was realized at the time, the situation was colored by the fact that a great many individuals and families were affected by mental and emotional disturbances among either persons rejected for the military or those who developed a service-related mental breakdown of some kind. In both groups, of course, for most of the men and women involved, the roots of their mental difficulty lay in destructive early experiences or harsh, negative community conditions, both urban and rural.

Such organizations as the National Committee for Mental Hygiene, founded in 1909, had been concerned with mental health problems for years. However, it was not until the development of modern techniques of mass communication that the public as a whole became aware of the dramatic prevention and cure potential of contemporary mental health programs. In turn, this broad-based support gave rise to appropriate legislation, along with the establishment and funding of a variety of national, state, and local nonprofit institutions for three key mental health thrusts: research, training, and services.

The last thirty years have seen extremely gratifying developments in the area of mental health. As an example, for patients who require hospitalization, there are five types of facilities now available, many of them in localities and regions which were largely devoid of them a generation ago. These include: large state hospitals, VA mental hospitals, small psychiatric hospitals, psychiatric units of general hospitals, and the in-patient services of community mental health centers. Accompanying these developments have been significant advances along three major lines: psychotherapy, rehabilitative therapy, and physiological methods. Additionally, although admissions to mental institutions continue to increase, the number discharged or treated on an outpatient basis grows with each passing year—a great tribute to modern approaches to mental illness.

Today, adequate mental health care has "come of age." Increasingly, like physical care, emotional equilibrium is being recognized as every citizen's right. Not only are we becoming accustomed to the premise of public responsibility for welfare and social security systems, but also to prepayment and insurance plans to ease the burden of individual or family medical expenses, including that incurred for mental illness.

A recent conference on rehabilitation concluded on the note that, as a field, it will continue its astonishing rate of increase through the decade of the 1980s. Two political conditions, they found, have thrust rehabilitation onto the medical arena's center stage: advances in science and the ethic of public concern. To a society like ours, with an ideology rooted in religious and humanistic traditions, the growing number of mentally ill individuals represents an important public concern and challenge.

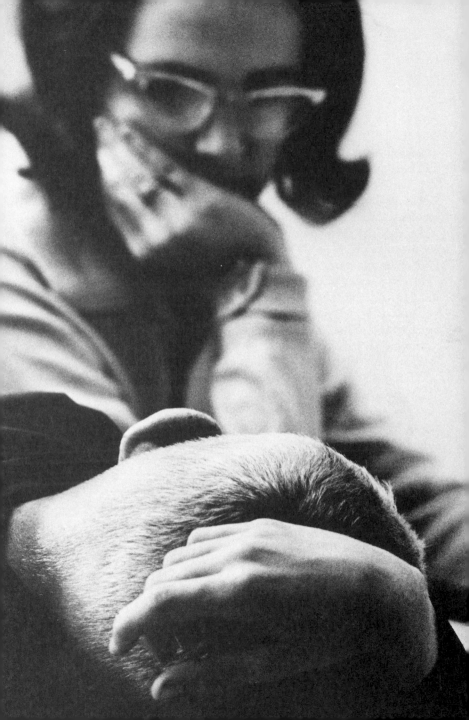

CHAPTER 2

WHAT IS MENTAL ILLNESS AND
HOW DOES A PSYCHIATRIST TREAT IT?

As was stated earlier, psychiatry is that branch of medical science which is concerned with the identification, analysis, treatment, and cure of mental illness, as well as its prevention. Traditionally, mental illnesses are classified into one of two types—organic or functional (which sometimes overlap). Organic mental illnesses usually arise from physical causes, i.e., defects in or damage to the human nervous system, especially the brain. Functional mental illnesses, on the other hand, usually occur as a result of psychological damage of some kind. Both types of mental illness, or their various combinations, can range in seriousness from mild to severe and in treatability from excellent to hopeless, depending on the state of medical science's knowledge and the willingness (or capability) of the patient to be cured.

A comprehensive definition of "mental illness" would be very difficult to make for a variety of reasons. For one, the scope of both organic and functional mental illness is quite broad; entire books can be devoted to a single aspect of a particular type of disease. Secondly, cultural considerations further complicate such a definition; what may be "normal" in one culture may be "abnormal" in another culture, or what may have been "abnormal" in the past may be "normal" now, or vice versa. Therefore, only the broadest definition of "mental illness" can be attempted to cover all possible conditions.

Such a definition might be: that state of mind in an individual which produces behavior so significantly different from that specified as "normal" by the current standards of his particular society that he ceases, for whatever reasons, to function effectively either as an individual human being or as a member of his society. Here again, "effectively" is a troublesome word. For example, a person suffering from a pathological fear of wide open spaces (agoraphobia) to the extent that he experiences anxiety when he crosses broad city boulevards would necessarily be considered mentally ill by such a definition. Yet even Sigmund Freud, the father of psychoanalysis, suffered from exactly this condition and yet managed to function effectively all of his life. Thus, it is nearly impossible to define mental illness in an all-inclusive sense. Instead, psychiatrists frequently rely on generalized definitions of mental *health* to help them identify mental *disease*, as deviations from the norm. One such recent definition of mental health, issued by the prestigious and influential American Psychiatric Association (APA), is:

> "A state of being, relative rather than absolute, in which a person has effected a reasonably satisfactory integration of his instinctual drives. His integration is acceptable to himself and his social milieu as reflected in his interpersonal relationships, his level of satisfaction in living, his actual achievement, his flexibility, and the level of maturity he has attained."

Another such definition, by the Joint Commission on Mental Health of Children, is:

> "The mentally healthy individual thus becomes one whose private life is evaluated against such somewhat vague but still highly meaningful concepts as integrity, authenticity, and self-determination, and

whose relationships with others may be judged in the light of such notions as effective intimacy in love and friendship, contributory participation in the affairs of a community, and the breadth of his sympathy with others whose backgrounds of experience differ from his own."

Both of these definitions stress the ability of the "mentally healthy" person to function effectively and happily in the various social roles of his culture. Though they may over-emphasize "adjustment" to arbitrary social conventions, at least they enable us to focus on what mental health should be and how to help those who deviate from the norm. However, the historical and cultural biases of any definition of mental health or illness must constantly be borne in mind. The witch trials of 17th century Europe and America were only one example of how torture and murder can be justified in the name of social, religious, political, or other cultural "norms."

TYPES OF MENTAL ILLNESS

As mentioned above, the psychiatrist may be called upon to treat either organic or functional mental illness. Inasmuch as organic diseases are infinitely more technical in concept and vocabulary, this discussion will be restricted to more commonly understood functional diseases—those with predominantly psychological, rather than physiologic, origins.

Functional mental illnesses are divided into three general categories: *psychoneuroses, psychoses,* and *personality disorders.*

Psychoneuroses. If you consider normal behavior to be at one end of the spectrum of human behavior and abnormal behavior at the other end, behavior in the middle portion is considered to be *psychoneurotic*—not entirely normal, but not obviously abnormal either. Psychoneurotic personality patterns are distinguished from seriously abnormal personality patterns (*psychoses*) by the fact that outlook for their cure, or at least reasonable adjustment, is fair to excellent. *Phobias,* such as Freud's agoraphobia, are psychoneuroses, as are such *compulsions* as avoiding cracks in sidewalk pavements. *Diffuse anxiety* (fear and nervousness for no apparent reason) or the milder forms of recurring depression are also classifiable as psychoneuroses. The important factor in distinguishing a psychoneurosis from a psychosis is, again, the severity of the irrational behavior involved.

Psychoses. The psychotic patient exhibits personality and behavioral disorganization which is vastly more complicated than that of psychoneurotic patients. During the acute phases of their illnesses, psychotic patients must be relieved of their normal responsibilities and removed from their familiar environments. *Manic-depressive psychosis* is characterized by alternating periods of *mania* (frenzy) and *melancholia* (extreme mental depression). *Involutional melancholia* is regarded as an emotional side effect of the menopause, and *depressive state* (or a depressive reaction) is common among elderly patients. *Acute depression* may develop in a moderately neurotic person who encounters a crisis of some kind which overpowers him.

Schizophrenia is the most common form of psychosis, accounting for half the cases. *Process schizophrenia* is the result of gradual deterioration and cure is unlikely. *Reactive schizophrenia* is the result of severe conflict or a traumatic happening; prognosis for recovery from this malady is good. Basic symptoms are withdrawal from reality, delusions, erratic thought, and the like. Heredity and childhood experiences are believed to be causal factors. Childhood schizophrenia is characterized by autistic behavior, that is, withdrawal from reality and human contact. Treatment concentrates on patient socialization, sometimes supplemented by drugs.

Paranoia. When suffering from paranoia or paranoid reaction, an individual is obsessed with a set of delusions. These may be delusions of grandeur, of persecution, or false belief that objects or situations which are totally unrelated to him or her have special significance.

The prognosis for psychotic personalities (who, incidentally, are frequently involuntarily hospitalized) is not always as good as for psychoneurotic personalities. In psychotic patients, contact with reality is at a minimum, as is interest in, or capability for, total cure.

Personality disorders. These reveal their presence through patterns of behavior rather than by emotional or physical manifestations. Those afflicted do not have the suffering of the psychoneurotic although the disorder can be most destructive to relationships with others. There are three main categories:

a) Disturbances of personality pattern. Failure to attain any kind of emotional, economic, occupational, and social adjustment.

b) Disturbances of personality traits. Any of a variety of emotionally unstable personalities often characterized by passive-aggressive behavior.

c) Disturbances of sociopathic personalities. A sociopathic personality strives consciously and guiltlessly to be offensive and not to act according to society's established ways. He or she often commits acts of violence, may also be an alcoholic or drug addict—although the latter are not sociopaths *per se.*

Prognosis for persons with personality disorders varies with the individual. Unlike the psychotic personality, which is clearly "abnormal," or the psychoneurotic personality, which is comparatively harmless, those with personality disorders may have very subtle pathological problems which are potentially quite dangerous to society. They are unhappy and ill enough to need psychiatric help, but seldom seek it and are only referred for treatment after its need has already manifested itself, sometimes in criminal or near-criminal acts.

TREATMENT OF MENTAL ILLNESS

Treatment of mental illness varies because of the infinite variety and intensities of disorders. There are, furthermore, few ways to evaluate its efficiency; treatment helps some patients a great deal, others a little, and a few, not at all.

The following are only some of the healing techniques employed by psychiatrists: psychotropic drugs; electroconvulsive therapy; carbon dioxide therapy; individual psychotherapy; psychoanalysis; behavior modification; group psychotherapy; training laboratory and sensitivity training; psychodrama; sociomilieu programs; family therapy; crisis intervention through psychiatric emergency rooms and walk-in clinics; and alcoholism and drug dependency clinics and programs.

Out of this rather impressive listing, we shall examine some of the more common therapeutic methods used by the psychiatrist.

Psychoanalysis. This approach has been greatly influenced by Freud's view that most emotional problems stem from a conflict between the patient's conscious self and his unconscious. In normal individuals, these conflicts are resolved. In the case of a mental patient, the analyst endeavors to uncover repressed conflicts and unconsciously stored frustrations which have caused psychological maladjustments. The therapist may meet with the patient in hour-long sessions fairly frequently, sometimes as often as three times a week. During these sessions, the therapist endeavors to make the individual aware of his unconscious motives and uncover the source of his conflict and his reasons for repressing it.

The psychoanalyst tries to guide the general drift of the conversation but to remain subtle about it. He might employ the technique of *free association,* which may elicit a flow of words or stories from which the analyst may piece together the patient's unconscious. Reports of the patient's dreams may give the analyst insight into unconscious motives. The whole process of psychoanalysis often is made difficult by the patient's tendency to continually repress key thoughts or ideas. At the same time, of course, this very "forgetfulness" may indicate that a solution lies ahead. Similarly, the concept of *transference* (for example, regarding the doctor as an object of fear or as a father image) may further the physician's insights, with a resulting clarification of the patient's problems and often some of the early personal relationships which underlie those problems.

Some therapists use *client-centered* or *nondirective therapy* in which the patient is encouraged to talk about himself. The focus is on current problems with the objective of the patient's "talking through" his troubles in order to become increasingly self-confident and self-reliant. *Directive therapy* is quite different in that the analyst tries to treat specific behavior. For example, indecisiveness may be treated by leading the patient to undertake roles involving increasing responsibility.

Hypnosis or hypnotherapy is a useful device under certain conditions. After hypnosis is induced, the therapist may be able to use suggestion to eliminate mild disorders. The patient's recollection of past incidents often reveals suppressed conflicts which have led to subsequent maladjustments. Later, when the therapist and the patient can explore these together, not under the influence of hypnosis, there is a good chance that some of the current problems will disappear.

Not all therapy is done on a one-to-one basis. *Group therapy* is remarkably effective for some individuals, particularly the lonely and those lacking intellectual resources. Participants learn that their own problems are not unique and have been previously resolved by others. Groups like Alcoholics Anonymous and Synanon have proved rewarding for some, although quite ineffective for others. For those who are not afraid or reluctant to participate, the groups can be useful in developing poise,

In severe cases of certain illnesses, the patient may become catatonic, a condition characterized by immobility and muscular rigidity or inflexibility.

self-confidence, and the ability to relate to other people. *Family therapy* has evolved from the success of other kinds of group therapy. In this, the negative and harmful features of the family which have created psychological maladjustments can be examined, and intra-family communication can be improved, or in some instances, actually initiated for the first time.

Related to the preceding is *psychodrama,* or *role-playing,* in which patients either enact roles from their past or act out a situation which is pending and which worries or threatens them as, for example, a forthcoming job interview. Other resources to which the therapist may turn are *gestalt therapy* (helping the patient to study his current reactions and insights), *drug therapy,* plus a wide variety revolving around the utilization of music, dance, art, or play.

Shock therapy involves inducing a convulsion by passing (for a mere fraction of a second) an electric current across the frontal portion of the patient's cerebral cortex. This is followed by a brief period of unconsciousness. Shock treatment frequently leads to recovery from serious emotional disorders, most notably depression. Many experts feel it is best to use this technique in conjunction with psychotherapy.

Behavior modification is precisely what the term implies, "unlearning" maladaptive behavior in favor of that which is more appropriate in order to bring about corresponding and highly desirable changes in personality. It has much in common with "conditioning" in the manner of TV commercials which make you feel that if only you use a certain commodity, your life will be changed for the better, your popularity assured, and so forth.

Chemotherapy, involving the use of chemical substances—medicines—in the treatment of mental illness, is a comparatively new method that has attracted much interest and, in some circles, great support.

These are only some of the common therapeutic methods used by the psychiatrist. They, and others, are all directed toward satisfying the five principles essential to ensuring adequate national mental health care which were approved in 1972 by the American Psychiatric Association (APA). They are:

1. Psychiatric care is a concomitant of health care and must be provided to the same extent and at the same level as other types of health care.
2. Psychiatric care must be suited to the needs and characteristics of the patient (a full spectrum of treatment must be provided to meet diverse needs).
3. Protection of the rights of patients to privacy, confidentiality, and choice of treatment is essential.
4. Adequate safeguards such as periodic peer and utilization review of practicing psychiatrists to ensure both quality and appropriateness of care are a necessity.

5. Psychiatric care should be limited to active treatment of illness or disability.

For further information on mental illness and therapeutic methods, see APA's *A Psychiatric Glossary,* a superb reference work which will answer most of your questions and which is a good place to initiate any reading program.

CHAPTER 3

WHAT IS A PSYCHIATRIST?

Strictly speaking, a psychiatrist is a licensed physician who specializes in the diagnosis, treatment, and prevention of mental and emotional disorders. The psychiatrist's training generally encompasses undergraduate education at a pre-medical college or university, then medical education leading to a medical degree, followed by three or more years of approved residency training. For those who wish to enter a subspecialty, such as child psychiatry, psychoanalysis, or administration, still further training is required. As a doctor and specialist, a psychiatrist can prescribe and administer any type of therapy indicated, as well as drugs, medicine, surgery, or electroconvulsive shock therapy.

Medical psychotherapists may treat mental, emotional, and psychosomatic illness through a relationship with the patient in an individual, group, or family setting. Medical psychotherapy always entails continuing medical diagnostic evaluation and responsibility; it may be carried out with drug and other physical treatments. Medical psychotherapy assumes that the psychological and physical components of an illness are intertwined. At any point in the disease process, psychological symptoms may give rise to, substitute for, or occur with physical symptoms, and vice versa.

Non-medical psychotherapy may be carried out by psychologists, social workers, nurses, pastoral counselors, and other professionals with special training. Ethically, morally, and legally, however, these latter specialists must remove themselves from the situation when a medical approach is needed.

Besides being a licensed physician, a psychiatrist is also a human being, a professional person, and a citizen. In the remainder of this chapter we will examine the psychiatrist in these other capacities in terms of personal qualities that are desirable, professional and ethical standards that must be followed, and social goals achievable through the successful practice of psychiatry. A brief section on allied specialists follows this discussion.

THE PSYCHIATRIST AS A HUMAN BEING

Some desirable personal characteristics in a psychiatrist would include the following:

Interest in Other People. To start with the feature most crucial to a career in psychiatry, by far the most important consideration is: Have you a genuine interest in and a realistic knowledge of mankind, coupled with sympathy for others, including those with quite different backgrounds, interests, and ways of behavior? Are you prepared to work with those who need you as a professional psychiatrist? Do you possess the qualities of selflessness and dedication? Do you, moreover, have sufficient interest in others to be content and fulfilled in a psychiatry career? Do you care enough about others? Do you really feel that "all men are brothers"? Do you agree with John Donne that "no man is an island"? Do you have the necessary social sensitivity to understand a patient's illness and then treat it in the most effective fashion? Do you care enough to accept and appreciate in your patients and colleagues differences in behavioral styles, understandings, ideologies, and social habits?

The three "I's." It follows that those who succeed in psychiatry must first ask themselves if they possess these three "I's": *I*nterest, *I*dealism, and *I*ngenuity. Think of yourself for a moment. Do you have the interest, the curiosity, and the

Psychiatrists often work in a variety of settings to prevent mental health problems as well as to treat them.

ability to project yourself into another, all of which are required to be effective in psychiatry? What about the extent of your idealism? Is it adequate? Will it carry you through the difficult years of medical school and subsequent training? Are you more interested in helping others than in making money? Psychiatry, it must be realized, is lucrative; however, it is nowhere near being so much so as some of the other medical specialties. Finally, a feeling of frustration will be your lot if you cannot draw on ingenuity as a facet of your character. You may need a variety of approaches to each patient's unique set of problems. You must be able to grapple with each patient's individual situation and to consider all the likely causes of his illness.

After reading the above summary of the three basic "I's," use them as a yardstick to measure yourself as a potential psychiatrist.

Still keeping the above in mind, analyze your capacity for *listening*. The most important way to overcome our sometimes limited insights into mental illness is to study carefully each patient in order to determine the underlying problems. At all times, it is essential to have four "ears"—one with which to listen to what is being said; one to attend to what is not being said; one to hear how it is being said; and one to heed the unexpressed feelings. (Fern Lowry).

Determination. You may think you want to help people, but it may be more than you can stand! It might be overly burdensome for you to spend many long hours each week wrestling with other peoples' problems in their tense, concerned presence. Do you really want to work sufficiently hard to understand and help other people? With the above understood, are you positive that you find helping others sufficiently satisfying emotionally to keep you content and successful? Will it always enhance your own self-image to be helping others and to have them depending upon you for support and understanding? Is feeling "needed" a sufficient satisfaction for you—one which will carry you over the many inevitable rough spots in a long professional career?

Scholarship. Are you ready and willing to spend the long hours, assume the heavy burden of study and clinical preparation, and devote a number of years to preparing yourself for such a career? Do you have the determination to persevere in the face of the inevitable difficulties and obstacles? In view of the depth and duration of the necessary preparation, do you have the fundamental qualifications as a student, so that the lifelong role of scholar which psychiatry requires will be a congenial one for you? Do you have a questing mind? Are you a compulsive reader with that love of the printed word which obliges you to read whatever is around you, even the label on the bottle of Worcestershire sauce if there is nothing else at hand? Can you be a good student not only during your years of formal preparation but subsequently as well, remaining so entranced by your profession that you read regularly and deeply in its literature? Can you continue to seek new therapeutic formulae and techniques? Will you be able to remain cheerful in the face of stacks of research reports and articles, not to mention meeting the requirements of continuing education programs and, possibly, re-licensing?

Every individual is worth helping or curing. Do you believe this? Do you accept the idea that every person has the right to his or her own views, decisions, and lifestyle? Can you remember at all times to do something *with* and *for* the person you are helping—as opposed to something *to* the individual? In other words, can you maintain a relationship with your patient which rests on mutual trust? Can you always serve the needs of the patient, regardless of any personal opinions you may have about him?

Toughness. Like other professions, that of psychiatry requires for effectiveness and self-confidence a considerable measure of *toughness.* Do you have it? Examining this a bit closer, what do we find? There are a number of attributes which comprise this toughness, including the following:

- Faith and tenacity in your beliefs
- Capacity for decision-making combined with willingness both to change your mind and to seek help and advice from others
- Consistency
- Courage
- Flexibility in changing jobs or assignments
- Continuing self-analysis to determine, for example, your impression on others and adherence to professional objectivity.

THE PSYCHIATRIST AS A PROFESSIONAL

Discipline. An appropriate amount of self-restraint is essential for a career in psychiatry. It helps if you keep reminding yourself that luck or fate has played a role in your progress; that not all of it results from your being better than those with whom you are in competition. Can you keep yourself under control throughout your career?

Trustworthiness. You must be able to act with both associates and patients so that you consistently inspire their trust and confidence in you. You owe this much not only to yourself but to others, so that you are more effective, and thus more helpful. Can you visualize yourself in such a responsible role?

Ability to Lead. It follows from the objective of increasing your effectiveness, that you should develop yourself as a leader. Both as a student and as a doctor, you should consciously conduct yourself so that you are, in effect, a person of influence and ever-increasing prominence. Your stature in the profession will be measured not only by your skills but also by your ability to influence and lead others. You will find that by pushing yourself into ever-increasing and more demanding roles and situations, you will develop courage and resolution. You can utilize this in future situations when a great deal may be required of you. Can you so drive yourself?

Modesty. As you consciously strive to make your way in the psychiatry profession, will you be able to keep in mind that neither you nor your associates are perfect? Will you be able to cultivate the humility and intellectual integrity necessary to accept the fact that a certain measure of luck has played a role in the success you have enjoyed or will achieve?

Tact and Diplomacy. As a doctor and as a psychiatrist, you will need to cooperate with those with whom you work with a maximum degree of effectiveness and efficiency. You must be able to establish good—or at least, proper—personal and professional relationships with both your superiors and subordinates. Well-developed interpersonal skills are at a premium in the profession of psychiatry.

Decision-making ability. Can you take care not to act in such haste that you fail to see your problem and the issues involved in it clearly, with all of its dimensions and interrelations considered? On the other hand, can you give a response to a problem without unnecessary delay when action is clearly required? Immediate action may be called for in connection with a patient's diagnosis or treatment, in changing your job or professional affiliation, or in taking a decisive step in your personal life, such as divorcing an incompatible spouse. Will you be prepared to make such decisions over and over again throughout your career?

Loyalty. Loyalty belongs to those who have earned it, who have some reason to feel they deserve it, or who, at least in the eyes of the world, might appear to be entitled to it. Can you select such individuals with due care and maintain allegiance to them, even during difficult periods?

Choice of Spouse. Careful selection of a spouse—one who will "wear well" and be of assistance in every aspect of your personal and professional life—is critical. Such men and women are not easy to locate; but in view of the importance of this matter, it is highly desirable that you not hurry into your mate-selection process.

Self-Education. Can you make it a matter of the highest priority to maintain your professional knowledge in the face of the inevitable torrent of new scientific and medical breakthroughs? Some of these may well cause you to modify or abandon familiar concepts and approaches. In addition to improving your effectiveness, new discoveries will also help you keep up-to-date in your chosen field and to qualify for re-licensing, if necessary. It is to be hoped that in keeping up-to-date with the evolution of psychiatry, you will take on the sentiments of William Cowper, who said: "Knowledge is proud that he has learn'd so much; wisdome is humble that he knows no more."

Tenacity. Even though it may be a difficult period in your professional career, will you strive to focus on the job at hand as a beginner? Can you be diligent even if your first assignment may not be the most interesting or may even lack prestige? You should accept such tasks with minimal concern, aware that in most professions there are certain levels of responsibility which are habitually assigned to those without seniority.

Patience. Do you accept the fact that ours is a most imperfect world? It will be most helpful for you to acknowledge this without dismay or frustration. Our society, for example, is characterized both by love and hate; justice is achieved through force or threats of punishment. You must acknowledge that even so, there is occasional failure—that ours is a world in which both individuals and society as a whole must, from time to time, deal with the violent, the anti-social, even the senseless.

Optimism. Throughout your career, even as early as your high school and college days, it will be most helpful for you to maintain a high degree of optimism in your thinking and planning. Can you sustain this? It is a desirable and positive force to refuse to allow yourself to be engulfed in lengthy periods of pessimism or depression. Your career will progress more evenly; the amount of good you can accomplish for your patients will be increased.

Tolerance. The psychiatrist should not employ artificial tolerance, hoping thus to win over and to help the patient. Instead, it is essential to cultivate a constructive friendliness. The famous psychiatrist, Karen Horney, once described this process as one "in which recognition of certain deficiencies does not detract from the capacity to admire good qualities and potentialities." In other words, look for the good traits in everyone. Such insight increases the effectiveness of both the psychiatrist and the prescribed treatment of the patient.

Cultural relativity. This means that the successful psychiatrist must be aware of cultural norms and their hold on us all.

For example, even today, some families feel that it is more important for sons to be well educated than it is for daughters. Such a daughter, when a patient, may herself fail to recognize this discrimination. If the psychiatrist also does not identify it as an element in the situation, then the patient's problems may not be seen in the round.

Transference. The psychiatrist must constantly strive to refine this valuable therapeutic tool. Transference is a reproduction of emotions relating to repressed experiences and a replacement of another person (the psychiatrist) for the original object of the repressed impulses. Briefly, observation, understanding, and discussion of emotional reactions with the patient are a good approach to resolving mental ills. Everything patients reveal gives valuable insights into their problems and their cure, no matter how remote or irrational the revelations may appear. The psychiatrist must endeavor constantly to obtain detachment, maintain objectivity, and be aware of such patient problems as anxiety or insecurity. If, for example, the patient is falling in love with the psychiatrist, it is probably related to a much earlier relationship, and the matter must be painstakingly studied. The best way to discuss it with the patient must be carefully determined in order to make it an insightful matter and not a dead end.

Flexibility. For each kind of illness, the successful mental healer must keep an open mind about what kind of institution or therapeutic environment is best for each patient. David H. Clark has written, in his 1974 *Social Therapy in Psychiatry* and elsewhere, that a period in an institution can serve as a "living-learning" experience during which an individual actually can grow and increase in effectiveness. While one patient might benefit from one type of therapeutic environment, another might suffer under the same conditions.

Acceptance. The therapist must never neglect the "army" of those who need mental treatment or care but who are unattractive, disadvantaged, inarticulate, and are either crowded into outpatient clinics or "warehoused" in state hospitals. Obviously, it is much more congenial for psychiatrists to concern themselves with "YAVIS patients"—those who are *Y*oung, *A*ttractive, *V*erbal, *I*ntelligent, and *S*uccessful. As such, these patients usually are congenial and have a good chance of recovery. Both from a medical and a social standpoint, the former group of less attractive, less articulate patients presents a far greater challenge and deserves more attention than it usually receives.

Imaginativeness. The imaginative therapists encourage the use of a wide variety of allied health and preprofessional support personnel. The following have, along with others, repeatedly demonstrated their utility in various mental health situations: physician's assistants, nurses, aides, physical or occupational therapists, and foster parents or grandparents.

Professionalism. Therapists who hope for professional success and peer recognition must identify and develop those attributes which are expected in all specialties with a reputation for social prestige. The qualities to be demonstrated in both professional and personal contacts include: professional competence; social understanding; positive personality characteristics (as opposed to those which might inhibit skillful practice); a continuing thirst for up-to-date knowledge and skills; and an interest in research and teaching. Additionally, the psychiatry profession assumes and expects compliance with accepted ethical principles which frequently are higher and more idealistic than those of business or politics. Of course, an interest in people which transcends their frequent un-likeability, hostility, refusal to cooperate, or the like, is considered essential.

Furthermore, psychiatrists must always endeavor to strengthen the status of their profession and do nothing that might hurt it. Additionally, psychiatrists must work diligently to enhance the profession's public image, status, and techniques, as required by changing times and future needs. It is important for the extremely sensitive subject of psychiatry to enjoy society's approval. Society gives psychiatrists control over the education and admission policies pertaining to new psychiatrists. Psychiatrists must act as professional watch-dogs, always keeping in mind that individual interests are less important than the nation's needs. If there are not enough psychiatrists, efforts must be made to increase the number. Somehow the profession's expertise must be stretched so it meets more of the public's demands, possibly by incorporating additional allied health workers and other support personnel.

Desire to Excel. There is, of course, a great deal to be said for ambition and the satisfaction of professional recognition. So long as ethical considerations are observed, there is no reason why psychiatrists cannot satisfy their various personal objectives. There is nothing wrong with money, security, power, challenge, fun, adventure, and professional and community recognition. Actually, the harder psychiatrists work and the more they do for their patients and fellow practitioners, the more likely it is that they will enjoy all of these legitimate rewards.

Trustworthiness. Its importance warrants our mentioning a very sensitive area: *confidentiality.* As part of the therapeutic process, the psychiatrist must ask the patient to volunteer information not lightly divulged, perhaps involving facts which, if known, might be extremely damaging to others. The community and our laws regard this material as privileged information. Psychiatrists, even in such other roles as researchers, teachers, novelists, spouses, or parents, must never permit any breaches of confidentiality.

Willingness to explore. Within the ranks of psychiatry, there has been a traditional disdain for administrative and planning assignments. There has been a suggestion that these activities, even when they are completely involved with psychiatric programs or organizations, are diverting psychiatrists away from activities which are more important or somehow more "legitimate." It is highly desirable for the future of psychiatry, for its continuing public esteem, and for its ability to accomplish the mission assigned it, that psychiatrists abandon such a head-in-the-sand attitude. It is important that planning and administration be controlled by members of the profession. Only in this way can high standards be maintained. Without such control, there is danger that there will be a failure by the psychiatrists themselves to accept responsibility for their share of the emerging problems of society, both now and in the future. Rhetoric is not enough; there must be group action and involvement to justify the prestige, the financial rewards, and the autonomy bestowed upon psychiatry and its practitioners by society and undergirded by public opinion, laws, and statutes.

THE PSYCHIATRIST AS A CITIZEN

The training and general orientation of psychiatrists affects the manner in which they fill roles as professionals, citizens, wage earners, wives/husbands, and parents. The work of psychiatry directly touches those it treats and indirectly affects the patients' employers, co-workers, friends, neighbors, and family members. Increasingly, psychiatrists and those with whom they work cooperate to make a specific community into a place where the mentally ill can find help, care, or cure readily available.

Psychiatrists are acutely aware of the impact of social factors on mental health. They are conscious of the beneficial effects, for example, of happy, child-centered families and homes, on the one hand; on the other, they acknowledge the harmful effects of slum living, inadequate nutrition, emotional insecurity, and unemployment. As individuals, as citizens and voters, as members of a wide variety of groups and organizations, psychiatrists work to make ours a more vital and democratic society. Perhaps more than most citizens, possibly even more than some of their fellow physicians, they are attuned to change—and its response to human thought and action.

Psychiatrists are acutely concerned with beneficial social change, with the general improvement of social, economic, and political conditions, with more and better education for all members of our citizenry, with family stability, and with more effective ladders for social mobility. However, except for a few extremists, psychiatrists as a whole prefer to work within the system and to effect desirable social change as individuals and as organized professionals.

Whatever their lifestyle and political preferences, psychiatrists are keenly aware of the harmful effects that socioeconomic factors can have upon the disadvantaged, as opposed to those with numerous choices or alternatives to life's opportunities. Obviously, the able and the wealthy can make mistakes, pass up opportunities, and still have alternatives. We know that family background and income are key determinants for many dimensions of later life and that, to a considerable extent, depressed neighborhoods, communities, states, and regions have a negative influence. For example, low family income may mean abandonment by a parent, thus denying the children a model of a cohesive family unit. Inadequate food and poor nutrition may produce prematurity at birth, retardation in physical, mental, and social development, a higher incidence of illness, lethargy, and other characteristics which delay or prevent the development of full potential. Poor housing not only demoralizes, it makes proper rest and attention to homework almost impossible. Slums tend to have poor schools and often are characterized by crime, drugs, prostitution, and other deviant behavior. Healthy attitudes towards oneself, society, schooling, and the future are not encouraged in slum youngsters or, for that matter, in their parents, other relatives, or friends. Minority status (including being female) and discrimination can result in a low self-image (actually self-hate in many individuals), which in turn prevents full access to many institutions and services that would help a person to acquire a good education and a rewarding job.

Seeing at first hand the harm and human waste that a discouraging social and family environment can have upon our citizens, many psychiatrists hope and work for an American society with as many options for the poor as for those economically more fortunate. A few are concerned about the tensions deriving from a new gap between increasingly higher levels of educational preparation and a fairly restricted number of job opportunities with scope, challenge, and the full utilization of an individual's interests, values, and skills.

ALLIED SPECIALISTS

This chapter's overview of the psychiatrist would be incomplete without a brief look at some of his colleagues. These include:

The *psychoanalyst,* usually a psychiatrist, but always with an M.D. degree, is one who has had training in psychoanalysis and who employs the techniques of psychoanalytic therapy. The psychoanalyst may either practice psychoanalysis only or may utilize other approaches as well. Some clinical psychologists and psychiatric social workers do, in effect, practice psychoanalysis. There is always a feeling, however, that psychoanalysis is best, and most safely, conducted by a person with a medical background.

Psychoanalysis is a theory of the psychology of human development and behavior, a method of research, and a system of psychotherapy, originally developed by Sigmund Freud. Through analysis of free associations and interpretation of dreams, a patient's emotions and behavior are traced to the influence of repressed instinctual drives and the resulting defenses against them in the unconscious. Psychoanalytic treatment seeks to eliminate or diminish the undesirable effects of unconscious conflicts by making the patient aware of their existence, origin, and inappropriate expression in current emotions and behavior.

The *neurologist* is a physician with postgraduate training and experience in the field of organic diseases of the nervous system and whose professional work focuses primarily on this area. Neurologists also receive training in psychiatry. To look at it another way, they specialize in the brain and the nervous system, along with the psychological disorders that result from diseased or damaged tissue. The neurologist who practices psychiatry is called a neuropsychiatrist. As more and more is learned about the interplay between the mind and the body, the more desirable it may become to be proficient in neuropsychiatry.

The *clinical psychologist* does not have an M.D. degree but usually has earned a Ph.D. degree and has served an appropriate period of internship. Many clinical psychologists specialize in testing while others concentrate on behavior modification.

The *psychiatric social worker* usually has a master of social work degree and specializes in collecting information that will round out the psychiatrist's knowledge of the patient; or in assisting the patient first in understanding the treatment and secondly, in returning successfully and happily to family, community, and job. The psychiatric social worker also may maintain a private practice, functioning in similar fashion to a psychiatrist or clinical psychologist.

Despite the frequent, significant accomplishments of members of the last two professional categories, there may be limitations on what they can accomplish because of their lack of a formal medical background. They usually have less profes-

Music, art, and dance therapists, effectively combining artistic and scientific skills, are relatively new members of the mental health care team.

sional standing than the first two, their fees tend to be lower, and should they be asked to testify in court, their status and the resulting impact of their testimony are correspondingly less highly regarded.

As in other branches of medicine, the psychiatry team consists of *all* those who help the doctor, thus stretching his valuable, scarce skills. This approach also makes it possible to make use of the increasingly technological and complicated accomplishments which mark the wide gap between yesterday's psychiatry and that of the present.

Increasingly, members of the psychiatry team develop into specialists and professionals. As they become more proficient and more accepted, they assume many of the old responsibilities of the psychiatrist. However, the psychiatrist not only continues as their captain but is usually legally liable for what the team members do.

Teamwork is most striking in the growing area of allied health. Literally at the psychiatrist's elbow, one may find the *nurse,* the *social worker,* and the *pharmacist.* Others may include the *EEG technician* (the person operating the electro-encephalograph, a piece of equipment which detects, measures, and records brain waves, thus aiding in diagnoses of brain activity, even determining when legal death takes place), *aides, orderlies,* and *laboratory technicians.* We must also mention the clinic and hospital employees who keep what are frequently almost mini-towns operating for the benefit of the patients, staff, and visitors. These employees can be found in offices, in information centers, on switchboards, in kitchens, in laundries, in dental clinics, or in beauty parlors.

More and more, it has become recognized that the well-being of psychiatric patients is enhanced by both the patient-centered team and the larger, more diffused group of employees. After all, the doctor sees each patient for only a few minutes or an hour, perhaps once a week, but the nurses, aides, and orderlies virtually live with the mentally ill. When all of those working with patients are accepted as important in the lives of their charges, are given some voice and thoughtful responsibilities, a therapeutic environment is created in which a concerted effort is made to involve everyone in the treatment process. The current view is that the entire staff and patients themselves are, in effect, colleagues in the healing process.

These, then, are the colleagues and co-workers of the psychiatrist. But no better description of the psychiatrist and his life can be obtained than A. H. Chapman's *It's All Arranged, 15 Hours in a Psychiatrist's Life,* which uses the device of depicting one psychiatrist's long, fictional day to detail the various areas of mental illness that a doctor encounters. Additionally, he also touches on the problems faced by the medical profession and the community. The broad range he covers demonstrates that no capsule summary can include all the many hats a psychiatrist wears.

CHAPTER 4

EDUCATION FOR A PSYCHIATRY CAREER

To become a psychiatrist, you must first complete training as a physician, which means that you attend medical school and earn an M.D. degree. More so than for most other professions, it is essential to plan carefully for psychiatric education, from high school on through medical school. Medicine is a science which requires that its practitioners build solidly on a foundation of basic knowledge. Admission to a college pre-medical program depends to a significant extent on the excellence of your high school record as well as on what your teachers write the college admissions office about you. Much the same process of evaluation and analysis of you as a student and prospective doctor occurs when you seek admission to medical school, apply for internship or residency, and to some extent, when you set up practice and seek professional affiliations and memberships. Let's face it—your academic and co-curricular record and accomplishments follow you throughout your life!

HIGH SCHOOL

As early as possible, you should begin to study college and medical school catalogs in order to determine what courses you should take. You should complete all the requirements for admission, supplementing your program with courses which will help you with premed studies in college. Extra science classes, along with courses in the social sciences and subjects or activities which will assist in refining your communication skills would be particularly helpful.

Try to identify a person who can help you with questions and course selections. This might be your family physician or the local public health doctor. Some schools have a science teacher with a special interest in directing students toward science or medical careers. Additionally, your school's guidance counselors may be able to assist you by providing helpful reference material or catalogs.

Your community may have a Future Physicians Club or an Ars Medica Club sponsored by the local medical society. These organizations were established to attract outstanding students into medicine and to provide guidance for them. School science clubs and Medical Explorer Posts, sponsored by the Boy Scouts of America, also provide information about opportunities in the medical field. You might also want to read books and novels about physicians and the practice of medicine which are available in your school or public library.

COLLEGE

Selecting the best kind of undergraduate college for your premed course involves more than merely letting yourself be swept along into an institution which happens to be currently popular with your classmates. Medicine is such a competitive field that you should strive right from the very beginning to make your preparation one which will rival that of the other candidates.

Confine your consideration to undergraduate institutions with four years of course work. This means that you ignore community (junior) colleges unless pressing financial problems make it absolutely necessary that you spend a year or two at such an

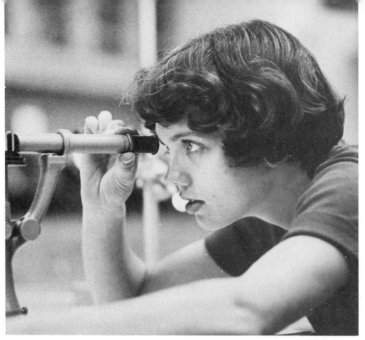

Science, social science, and language arts courses in high school are considered helpful to students planning a career in psychiatry.

institution prior to transferring. Be sure that the colleges you are considering are accredited by one of the six regional agencies of the American Council on Education.

Consider only those colleges which have consistently sent students to medical school and which have established premedical student advisory procedures. This may be an office, a committee, or a faculty member or administrator who is available to help you with your course selections and the complicated process and paperwork involved in applying to medical school. If the school you are considering does have such a preprofessional committee, it is almost certain that medical schools look with favor, or at least strong interest, on the college's graduates; that the college has a curriculum in the liberal arts tradition (as opposed to purely technical); that it offers the courses required for medical school, including good science courses and adequate laboratory facilities;

and that it has a reputation for high academic standards and a strong faculty.

Some undergraduate institutions with outstanding premed programs have arrangements with one or more medical schools which permit certain well-qualified students to enroll in enriched or accelerated programs, such as those in which the requirements for a medical degree can be completed in five calendar years immediately after high school. The first five terms are spent on the undergraduate campus, then the next two years at the medical school, with intervening periods of work for two summers back on the original undergraduate campus. Students must make application to such special programs while they are still in high school. Whether you desire a special program like this or a conventional one, it is essential to select a college whose curriculum and graduates are held in high regard by medical schools.

A few exceptional students are admitted to medical school with only 90 semester hours of undergraduate study, but preference generally is given to students who present a bachelor's degree reflecting a broad spectrum of courses. Understandably, admissions committees tend to be conservative and to prefer students with backgrounds which are broad but traditional. So, right from the start, plan your college curriculum with medical school in mind.

Almost all medical schools expect entering students to have completed a heavy load of natural science courses and to have gained a thorough grounding in the humanities and social sciences. Special course requirements vary from school to school; however, an undergraduate program which included at least the required and elective courses listed below would probably satisfy the admission requirements of most medical colleges:

English Composition and Literature
General Biology or Zoology (including laboratory)

Physics (including laboratory)
Inorganic Chemistry (including laboratory)
Organic Chemistry (including laboratory)

Of value to a medical student are such courses as: physical chemistry, quantitative analysis, comparative anatomy, genetics, embryology, calculus, psychology, sociology, and philosophy.

For further information about pre-medical preparation and admission to medical school, see *Medical School Admission Requirements.* This annually revised book is published by the Association of American Medical Colleges and includes information on:

- Planning a premedical education
- Factors to be considered in choosing a medical school
- The medical school admission process
- Financing medical education
- Opportunities for minority applicants
- The nature of modern medical education
- Factors to be considered for high school students interested in careers in medicine

All students interested in applying to medical school should consult this bulletin. A new edition is published in May of each year and is available at most medical schools, undergraduate college libraries, and in most pre-medical advisors' offices. Individual copies may be obtained by sending $5.00 to:

> *Medical School Admission Requirements*
> Association of American Medical Colleges
> 1 Dupont Circle N.W.
> Washington, D.C. 20036

MEDICAL SCHOOL

Application and Admission. Ideally, you should begin your

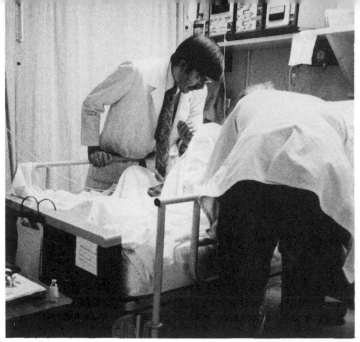

To become a psychiatrist, you must be willing to accept the rigorous challenge of medical school.

search for a medical school while you are still in high school. Your list should be well narrowed down by the time you get to college. Some medical schools publish brief brochures with titles like "Information for Prospective Students." Although these may not go into detail on courses or faculty members, they are invaluable for admission and examination requirements and deadlines.

At least a year prior to the beginning of the academic year in which you wish to enroll, you should apply to between four and ten medical schools. Well in advance of the announced deadlines, you must request application materials from the American Medical College Application Service (AMCAS) by writing to the Association of American Medical Colleges (One Dupont Circle N.W., Washington, D.C. 20036). Complete the forms they send you and return them to AMCAS, indicating to which medical schools you wish copies to be sent. Provide them with official transcripts and service fees as indicated. AMCAS will verify the information you provide and will then forward copies to the schools you have listed. As the medical schools receive their verified applications from AMCAS, each school sends you a packet of supplementary forms which it requires in order to complete your application file in their admissions office. Complete these as indicated and return them, along with the appropriate fees.

Act promptly on all admission steps and procedures. Remember that you are in competition with many others for places in medical schools. Early filing of applications makes possible optimum consideration and the correction of any errors or omissions. If you delay in completing application paperwork, there may be no vacancies when your admissions folder is finally completed. Even if it becomes tiresome, read all instructions and complete forms carefully.

It is likely that letters of recommendation will have to be sent to the various medical schools, either from the premedical committee at your college or from your science instructors. Remember that the preparation and mailing of these letters involve considerable time, effort, and sometimes, expense on the part of those preparing them. In every sense, when you ask someone to write a letter of recommendation, you are requesting a favor. Help by filling out those sections of the recommendation blank which you can do, such as your name, address, and social security number. By all means, provide postage and an envelope for the letter and form.

When you are filling out a blank or writing a statement, review it to make certain you have included all the required information. Always double check to see that you have answered every question, filled in every blank, enclosed all application fees, and enclosed stamped, addressed envelopes when they are required.

Entrance Examination. While you are in premedical college, preferably during your sophomore year but no later than your junior year, you must arrange to take a special medical aptitude test. In past years, this examination was called the Medical College Admission Test (MCAT); however, late in 1976, the Association of American Medical Colleges announced a totally new Medical College Admission Assessment Program (MCAAP) to succeed MCAT. MCAAP, which is approximately twice as long as its predecessor, was designed in part to eliminate the alleged racial and sexual biases of MCAT. To score well on this new test, applicants will need to have done well in undergraduate biology, chemistry, and physics courses. MCAAP includes a two-hour science section designed to test both knowledge and problem-solving ability. Further information about MCAAP can be obtained by writing to The Psychological Corporation, 304 East 45th Street, New York, N.Y. 10017.

Interviews. While medical school admissions committees would like to interview every applicant, the volume of applications they receive makes this impossible. Most medical schools attempt to interview some of the applicants, although an invitation to an interview is not necessarily an indication that you are likely to be accepted. Should you be invited for an interview, it is important that you make a good appearance and have ready answers to the questions and issues which are likely to come up during the discussion. The following are some of the most probable areas about which the committee will question you: the reason for your interest in medicine and how long you have had it; why you chose this particular medical school; your favorite college courses; any unusual features of your background or application blank comments; your plans for a medical specialty; whether or not you are married; and your interest in a physician-shortage area program, an armed forces scholarship, or a combined M.D.-Ph.D. program.

The main purposes of the interview, of course, are to enable the committee to familiarize itself with your appearance, intellect, ability to communicate, personal qualities, and motivation, as well as to familiarize you, the interviewee, with the school.

Even if the interview doesn't seem to be going well, do not be nervous; think before making your replies and be polite but not overly deferential. Remember that you should try to project yourself in such a way that the committee will remember you more vividly than the other candidates interviewed that day or week.

Early Decision Plan. You may have heard about the Early Decision Plan (EDP) whereby superior medical school applicants may request and receive early decision regarding their applications to the medical schools of their first choice. Application for such consideration must be made at least one year prior to the expected enrollment date, and students who are EDP candidates may not apply to any other U.S. medical school until the school of their first choice has made a decision on their admission. If they are turned down, application can then be made to other schools.

FOREIGN MEDICAL SCHOOLS

It is an unfortunate fact that each year, a great many highly qualified medical school applicants are passed over by American medical colleges. If you feel this is likely to happen to you, and if you feel that you have real talent and ability for medicine, can do the course work and ultimately pass the state and national board examinations, you should ask your advisers about the advisability of applying to a medical school in Canada, Mexico, or Europe.

A U.S. student who is determined to do so can receive a good medical education in a setting that is not traditional or, by our standards, not prestigious. Just as we make extensive use of foreign doctors in U.S. hospitals and communities (in fact, we could not operate many of our hospitals without foreign interns, residents, and staff physicians), so also do we accept native Americans who have been forced to study abroad because of limited medical school openings in the U.S. Moreover, at this writing, there are even federal financial aid programs for U.S. citizens who are studying abroad or who have returned to this country to complete their training after initial medical school attendance abroad.

It is not always easy to obtain information about medical study abroad; however, some foreign medical schools do have offices or representatives in the U.S. The Sunday *New York Times* carries advertisements of organizations and individuals who are available to assist students with applications to foreign medical schools. Do not hesitate to solicit information and references from these sources. Your college library and premed committee may also be helpful in this regard. On the other hand, some premed committees are reluctant to help with study abroad, so if you encounter resistance, do not be discouraged but push ahead on your own. Follow up leads in the newspaper and those you can locate in your library or vocational office.

LARGE VS. SMALL MEDICAL SCHOOLS

If you are interested in a career in psychiatry, you may wish to apply to medical schools with large departments of psychiatry and neurology. Your chances for obtaining the best preparation are most likely at the institutions which turn out a majority of U.S. psychiatrists, although it is certainly possible to obtain a good background for psychiatry at many small medical schools.

Let's look at the medical schools which have traditionally led in the production of psychiatrists and then discuss some of the advantages of psychiatry programs in large, as opposed to small, medical schools. A 1970 APA poll examined the medical school of origin of psychiatrists. Information from the 12,467 respondents revealed that the following 25 schools had graduated over 50 percent of the total:

Case Western Reserve University
University of Chicago
Columbia University
Cornell University
Hahnemann Medical Center
Harvard University
Indiana University
University of Illinois
Thomas Jefferson University
University of Maryland
University of Michigan
University of Minnesota
New York Medical College

New York University
Northwestern University
Ohio State University
University of Pennsylvania
St. Louis University
State University of New York
University of Tennessee
Temple University
University of Texas
Tufts University
Tulane University
Wayne State University

If you live in Canada or plan to study there, you should remember that the situation there is comparable. There were 440 graduates responding to the survey, and they represented 12 Canadian medical schools. Two of these schools, McGill and Toronto, accounted for more than 51 percent of the psychiatrists.

Psychiatry has become so complicated and specialized a profession that it is highly desirable to study at a medical school with a large psychiatric department or division. There appears to be a relationship between size and quality. Other things being equal, large organizations tend to attract strong, intellectually curious faculty members and students with provocative interests and local affiliations, as well as minority teachers and trainees. With size come recognition, greater diversity of programs, specialties, research grants and projects, publications, a wide range of courses, and a large budget.

In the larger programs, you are more likely than in smaller ones to profit from working with and learning from physicians in other disciplines and from allied health personnel and clinical specialists. Additionally, large programs often expose students to such social problems as poverty and racism, thus enhancing their skills development and preparation for general community practice.

INTERNSHIP AND RESIDENCY

If you have decided that you want to specialize in psychiatry or neurology, even before receiving your M.D., you must determine whether or not you wish to take a year or two as an intern. The internship and/or residency is the next screening process you must survive on your road to becoming a psychiatrist. In an extensive study of higher education which paid special attention to national health needs and problems, the Carnegie Commission on Higher Education concluded it would be highly desirable to shorten, from eight years to six, the length of time it takes after the receipt of the B.A. degree to become a practicing medical doctor. The decision was reached not only with an eye to improving medical education but also to help the current imbalance of national physician distribution. Various ways to accomplish this goal were suggested. The most obvious measure proposed is one to which you may well wish to give serious consideration. It was to eliminate the internship.

In the past, the internship was considered to be, if not essentially a fifth year of medical school, at least an integral part of the medical education sequence. Presumably, it supplemented formal instruction by giving a well-rounded experience of closely supervised clinical practice in diagnosis and therapy, accompanied by a progressive increase in the intern's responsibilities. Today, however, with the thoughtfully developed "clinical clerkships" of most medical schools and the expansion of residency training, more and more women and men are deciding to skip the internship period and move right into a residency. On the other hand, at this writing, some states still require an internship prior to license qualification. But more and more, the internship requirement is being abandoned in favor of accepting the first year of residency in its place. Medical schools, educators, and even legislators generally have gone along with most of the recommendations of the Carnegie Commission. Unless you feel your medical school background did not give you the professional skills and self-assurance you would like to have, you would probably be well advised to think in terms of going right into residency.

RESIDENCY

The establishment of formal residency programs goes back to 1933, when they were regularized by the American Medical Association (AMA) to train physicians in the specialty of psychiatry. The residency program in basic psychiatry is currently a three-year program of full-time training. The subspecialty of child psychiatry requires two or more years of specialized training; most residents in child psychiatry substitute the first year of child subspecialty training for the third year of adult residency for a total training period of four years. Thus a fully qualified psychiatrist is considered to have completed, as a minimum, a three-year basic residency program. Three years of such training are required for full membership in the American Psychiatric Association.

There is an invaluable reference which you should examine carefully as you decide about where to apply for admission to psychiatric residency training programs. Edited by Lee Gurel, M.D., it is entitled *A Descriptive Directory of Psychiatric Training Programs in the United States, 1972-73* (American Psychiatric Association). Equally important are the American Medical Association's *Directory of Approved Internships and Residencies* and the American Psychiatric Association's *Guide for Residency*

Programs in Psychiatry and Neurology. There are also other guides which may be available in your medical school's library.

In this connection, in 1973 the APA published another invaluable work which does not mention specific training facilities by name but which does explore the wide variation in emphases of the nation's programs for psychiatric residents. Also by Gurel, it is entitled *A Survey of Academic Resources in Psychiatric Residency Training.* The study dealt with 4,750 residents and found that most programs involved training for the standard three-year residency or for the three-year residency plus one or two years of advanced training. One interesting aspect of the report is the notion that if the number of residents is small, there is likely to be a lack of intellectual stimulation. Poor interaction, as a result of too few trainees, often contributes to a less than optimal residential training experience. You should certainly keep in mind this possible shortcoming and investigate the setting when applying for specific residency programs.

At the time the study was made, over a third of the students (37 percent) entered residency directly from medical school. Twenty percent had been out of medical school from two to three years; another 15 percent from four to five years. The rest had been out of medical school for between 6 and 15 years, and sometimes, even longer. Some of these were graduates of foreign medical schools; however, it is likely that a number were physicians who had originally pursued another specialty and then decided either to change fields or to broaden their expertise.

Another point to consider when planning residency training is how progressive or socially conscious each institution's philosophy seems to be. You should investigate such matters as:

- emphasis in your psychiatric training on community psychiatry centers and the achievement of new skills in community consultation, organization, and administration, in child advocacy, and in program evaluation;

• training of psychiatrists to deal with such critical social problems as drugs, alcoholism, poverty, and racism;

• training of psychiatrists to work collaboratively with paraprofessional personnel such as aides;

• the interdisciplinary aspects of psychiatric training;

• the extent to which minority trainees and faculty are recruited; and

• the program's concern with child mental health problems and techniques.

FINANCING COLLEGE AND MEDICAL SCHOOL

In this section we will examine the financial obligations you will assume in the four years leading to your bachelor's degree and the three subsequent years required for your M.D., treating them as a single block. Ideally, there should be no break between your college and medical school work, even though you may be tempted to work for a year after college in order to accumulate funds for further study. This is usually an unwise decision; it's likely that your savings for this period probably won't amount to much, and you will lose valuable momentum and the accumulated knowledge from pre-med course subject matter in the process.

You and your family should try to view educational expenses as an investment—money laid out for future profit and income. Too great emphasis cannot be placed on what a desirable investment it is. The skills you will master in college and medical school will create in you resources that will enhance your future earnings throughout your professional career, not to mention numerous incidental personal satisfactions.

There are two "cost" components: the earnings you might have made instead of studying, and the actual expenses of the education. In a 1972 report, the National Commission on Productivity concluded that those who complete college can expect an annual return of at least 15 percent on the total cost, and those who go on for further study, such as medicine, can expect an additional 15 percent. As a doctor, you can expect to receive hypothetical "dividends" on all of your studying costs from elementary school on up through medical school. With medicine currently the nation's best paying profession, you can see that even though the costs are high, they are an outstanding investment.

So, instead of being intimidated by the amount of money you will spend and the fact that you may have to assume some loans, think of the overall costs as being a sound financial investment. If you should feel yourself wavering, you might take a look at the chapter on the kinds of financial returns psychiatrists and other doctors enjoy. Hopefully, in another few years, you'll be experiencing the same kind of gratifying yearly income. Almost certainly, by then, it will be an even larger figure, as your gains keep pace with inflation. Even so, you must be sober and completely realistic in your financial planning. You must permit no wishful thinking to play any part in your deliberations and choices. How do you achieve such intelligent and creative insights into the financial side of your long and costly medical preparation?

It is absolutely essential, first of all, to sit down and determine the dimensions of your particular problem; to make some long-range financial plans; and to compose a budget. Keep in mind the effects of inflation, rising costs, and wages, which probably will characterize the rest of this century. By their very nature, colleges, universities, and medical schools are immediately subject to national increases in rising costs and wages. As a result, at this writing, in almost every section of the country, some of them are sliding into serious indebtedness. Others are closing their doors and going out of existence. You can be sure that the institutions which survive will be making realistic annual increases in student fees, probably on the order of 5-15 percent. In the following discussion, the three largest items of cost are tuition, room, and board. At some institutions, "fees" and "charges" have special significance; however because there is no standardized differentiation, in this chapter we use the terms fees, charges, costs, sums, and expenses interchangeably.

For starters, we'll look at some institutional room, board, and tuition charges. We'll examine institutional student costs at a sample of state universities; a cross-section of colleges identified with rural, black students; traditional liberal arts colleges; and a selection of medical schools. While you may be able to cut some corners on clothes and recreation, without some kind of scholarship or other aid, there is no way to sidestep payment of institutional charges for room, board, and tuition. The following are excerpted from the College Scholarship Services publication, *Student Expenses at Postsecondary Institutions 1976-1977.* If you can't locate the latest issue of this annual study in a library or counselor's office, you can order one from the College Entrance Examination Board (Box 2815, Princeton, New Jersey 08540).

First, let's take a look at some of the comprehensive charges for undergraduates at a few of our great state institutions. Their faculties, libraries, laboratories, physical plants, and student bodies are outstanding. Because of state support, they are able to keep their room, board, and tuition charges low, as shown by this sample:

University of Alaska at Anchorage	$4,400
University of California at Los Angeles	3,720
University of Connecticut	3,400
University of Delaware	3,102
University of Florida	3,105
University of Hawaii at Manoa	3,017

University of Kansas	2,875
University of Maine at Augusta	3,000
University of South Carolina	2,450
University of Texas	3,000
Texas Woman's University	2,500
University of Wyoming	2,520

Secondly, let's examine the costs at some of the fine institutions which have been identified with the preparation of many of our black leaders down through the years. Student charges at a sample of these are as follows:

Fisk University	$4,175
Hampton Institute	3,595
Howard University	3,854
Prairie View A & M University	2,991
Shaw University	3,450
Tougaloo College	2,780
Tuskegee Institute	3,000
Voorhees College	3,515

The last sample is from the more traditional, liberal arts-oriented, essentially residential, undergraduate institutions:

Amherst College	$6,300
Barnard College	6,300
Bates College	5,500
Colby College	5,200
Colorado Women's College	5,270
Dartmouth College	6,960
Drake University	5,060
Emory University	5,775
Furman University	4,707
Georgetown University	5,500
Harvard University	7,300
Harvey Mudd College	6,300

Lake Forest College	5,510
Mount Holyoke College	6,100
Rollins College	5,300
Simmons College	5,774
Swarthmore College	5,640
Trinity College (Connecticut)	6,000
Tufts University	6,800
Tulane University	5,600
University of Notre Dame	5,310
Williams College	6,300
Yale University	7,175

The medical schools in the following summary reflect regional differences and suggest the importance of evaluating financial requirements along with curriculum. The annual room, board, and tuition fees for a useful sample on which information was available as this chapter was researched are as follows:

University of Alabama	
Medical School at Birmingham	$2,960
University of California	
Medical School at Davis	4,825
Medical School at San Diego	4,993
Loma Linda University	
School of Medicine	5,150
University of Connecticut	
Medical School	5,255
Medical College of Georgia	2,464
Northwestern University	
Medical School	7,100
University of Illinois	
Medical Center	3,884
Indiana University	
School of Medicine	4,724

University of Iowa College of Medicine	4,285
University of Kansas Medical Center	3,130
Johns Hopkins University School of Health Services	6,625
University of Maryland School of Medicine	5,340
Boston University School of Medicine	4,903
University of Nebraska Medical Center	2,900
Albany Medical College	8,200
New York University School of Medicine	9,625
State University of New York Upstate Medical Center	3,800
Wake Forest University Bowman Gray School of Medicine	6,900
University of North Dakota School of Medicine	3,750
University of Cincinnati College of Medicine	4,175
University of Oregon Medical School	4,751
Hahnemann Medical College	8,500
University of Pittsburgh School of Medicine	7,100
Texas Tech School of Medicine	4,980
University of Washington School of Medicine	4,635

In planning your educational budget, it is imperative for you to keep in mind that the figures given in the summaries of institutional fees usually do not include books, supplies, laboratory fees, microscopes, graduation expenses, and miscellaneous other costs. Personal items and recreation are also extra.

There is no absolute correlation between student charges and the quality of the education you will receive. If you apply yourself conscientiously, it is possible to obtain a sound, basic education at any accredited college or medical school. However, it is important, as we emphasized earlier, to select an undergraduate institution with a good pre-med course and a reputation for sending its graduates on to medical school.

Why, you may well ask, are there differences in costs? Frequently, they result from proportionately lower costs of living, labor, and construction in certain sections of the country; or from a traditional interest in a particular group of regional or low-income students. Additionally, costs are affected by the amount of state and/or federal financial assistance a school receives. Another important cost factor is a school's emphasis on its concentration on teaching. Research is much more expensive to support than teaching. Endowments, contributions, and support from religious groups, alumni, and business also affect the fees charged by institutions of higher education.

As you view the prospect of an expensive medical education, you might be tempted to consider attending a community college or even taking correspondence courses to gain academic credit inexpensively. This kind of preparation may save money but also may fail to impress admissions committees unless you can make an extremely strong case for this approach to medical school. Admissions committees are swamped with applications, and they may discard with only brief examination applications from candidates whose preparations do not include four years at a traditional liberal arts college. On the other hand, if the admissions office has moved with the times, an unusual educational and employment backgrounds may actually work in your favor, especially if you have surmounted heavy odds to prepare for medical school, and have demonstrated your academic ability.

A SCHOOL BUDGET

It is essential to have an accurate, comprehensive budget. Only through careful planning can you be certain that you have some realistic idea of your needs and your financial outgo. A budget can act as a check on your expenditures, allowing you to spread your available funds over the academic years and billing periods and not exhaust them prematurely.

Before you develop a budget, you must have an abundance of valid information on which to base it. First, make a list of your likely financial needs; then, make a second one which summarizes the sources and amounts of funds you anticipate. Let's consider the first list—those items which represent expenses.

Expenses. To save space, we have combined into one summary the expenses of both the undergraduate years and medical school. Keep in mind that you cannot be certain about some of these expenses unless you have observed your spending characteristics over a number of months. If you are at present residing at home, try to visualize yourself as living independently. Your budget should include at least the following:

- Basic educational expenses
- Food and related items
- Recreational activities
- Health and personal care items
- Transportation expenses
- Clothes
- Household items
- Miscellaneous (insurance, gifts, etc.) and contingency (emergency travel, etc.) expenses

To allow for inflation, you should increase your estimates of what you will spend on each item by 10 percent each year.

Revenue. After you have determined your expenses, evaluate the most common sources of educational funds from your personal standpoint to determine how much money you can expect from:

• Savings from your previous summer jobs or money your parents have put aside for your education; gifts or loans from your family or friends.

• Diversion of some of the current earnings of the family to your educational expenses. How much can be spared at home?

• Your future vacation employment and other part-time jobs.

• Scholarships and fellowships, usually but not necessarily related to the college or medical school.

• Grants, gifts, and loans.

FINANCIAL AID

If you are sure you will need financial assistance, study college and medical school catalogs carefully to see what they have to offer and for any leads you should follow up. There is almost always an institutional blank for you to fill out. When you submit the blank, you initiate the financial aid process. This should be done as early as possible, in addition to filling out the CSS blank, which is discussed below.

Let's examine some points that a financial aid officer keeps in mind. Although there are some profit-making educational institutions in this country, as a premedical student or a medical student, your sole contact probably will be with non-profit making institutions. Such schools usually lose money on every student; they exist solely to perform a public service and manage to survive through the generosity of alumni, public contributions, and governmental support. As a result, they feel that prospective students and their families should do everything possible to pay for medical education without assistance. There are inadequate funds to be spread among all that seek them, and institutions are honor-bound to stretch them as far as possible among qualified applicants.

Additionally, financial aid officers are obligated to give assistance to those students who are most likely to complete the course. While students are not expected actually to pay back those funds which are awarded without strings, it is hoped they will someday make a corresponding contribution to society. While students receiving financial aid are assumed to be good bets to succeed, they are not necessarily expected to be at the very top of their classes at the time they apply for funds. What is required is better-than-average class standing and demonstrated seriousness of purpose, undergirded by "give-till-it-hurts" family support, both moral and financial.

It follows then, that you should do all that you can to project yourself and your need for assistance as truthfully as possible to the financial aid officer. Volunteer to provide all of the information needed or requested and do it promptly and cheerfully. If you should have some financial resources or awards that you have not yet disclosed to the institution, tell them about these matters. They will appreciate your frankness. Aid applicants and their families only hurt their own cases if they are reluctant to share details of family finances, resources, and dependents.

In all likelihood, the institution from which you seek help will think and act in terms of a scholarship, campus job, and/or a loan. The specific amount of financial aid you will receive from the institution is determined after you and your parents have reported all aspects of the family's financial picture to the institution and have filled out blanks for the College Scholarship Service (CSS), a division of the College Entrance Examination Board (CEEB). After analyzing the family's financial picture, including income and all assets, the Service recommends to the college the amount it feels the family should provide. The CSS sends the information to more than one institution if you so request, thus eliminating the need for you to duplicate facts.

More and more, colleges are beginning to feel that even families with gross incomes of from $15,000 to $25,000 should not be expected to provide all of the funds a daughter or son needs if the family has many other demands. These might include more than one child being educated, major illnesses, crippling business reverses, and the like. The CSS recommendation gives the college an idea of your needs and helps it develop your particular aid package.

Cooperative Education. Many Colleges have developed employment programs which are integrated with academic work. These cooperative education programs are developed in a variety of ways, from the simplest kind of employment assistance by the institution, up to and including an arrangement whereby you are paired with another student with whom you alternate work days on a paid job. In some cases, job duties are related to students' academic majors. Many work-study programs have federal support. In such cases, the federal government pays up to 80 percent of students' salaries for work in a hospital, school, on campus, or in a government-related project. Check this out with the campus placement office or the local Civil Service Commission. Most institutions can help you apply for a federally sponsored Basic Opportunity Grant (BOG). The bulletin boards of various campus offices and departments also are good sources for job information.

Scholarships. Keep in mind that most institutional scholarships are small, and many are actually appropriated from current income in recognition of the college's public obligations. Of course, some scholarships are endowed as memorials. A classified advertisement in a national magazine recently called attention to Vanderbilt University's $5,000 scholarships which are awarded "to students who have demonstrated qualities characteristic of Mr. [Harold Stirling] Vanderbilt" during their four years as undergraduates.

There are some scholarships which are earmarked for graduates for a certain school, those from a specific community, those majoring in a particular area, those with ancestors who served with the Confederate forces, or those whose parents work for a certain company. It does no harm to look into these awards, but the amounts are usually only between $100 and $500, and there are far too few to go to all those who qualify for or need them.

The most highly publicized scholarships are those of the National Merit Scholarship Corporation. These are awarded to the highest standing students but the money is given only to those with great financial need. If you rank high but do not require financial help, prestige is your only reward. However, high rank as a National Merit Scholar certainly helps you win acceptance to college. This recognition also makes you stand out from other scholarship applicants as being a person likely to excel.

Many states have programs of scholarship awards, often handled by the members of the legislatures themselves. They vary tremendously in value and in terms of the necessary qualifications for them. Family needs is *not* always a major factor. Whatever your circumstances may be, you would be well advised to write for information to your state senator, representative, or your state department of education.

Your school guidance office and library should have information about scholarships awarded by local or regional service clubs, labor unions, large regional industries, insurance companies, and other private sources. Check the list of suggestions at the end of this chapter for other possibilities.

Grants. This is the term preferred by some institutions for all kinds of scholarships and awards of aid, while other colleges and universities use the same word to describe aid supplements which are separate from those made possible by benefactors, alumni, or from annual appropriations by the institution itself. The most significant grant programs involve huge amounts of federal assistance spread out over many institutions and individuals. The sums of money change from year to year, even quarter to quarter, as demand and congressional appropriations vary. Their principal but not sole purpose is to enlarge and to make more diverse the nation's student body by assisting with the high costs of postsecondary educations.

Loans. Loans are a tangible way of investing in yourself; however, they strike some students as burdens they would prefer to avoid. On balance, the vast majority of American students who have received loans have been able to pay them off without undue hardship, except during the depth of the mid-1970s economic recession. At that time, there were some instances of defaults and public criticism of the few students who were seeking a way out by declaring bankruptcy. However, the concept of national student loan programs seems to have become an accepted part of our nation's economy. Many colleges and universities would suffer severe financial setbacks if the programs were terminated.

It may not be possible for you to obtain all your needed funds in the form of scholarships, loans, or grants. In that case, there is no alternative to going to a bank and borrowing the money. The rates may seem high, particularly if there is little likelihood of your paying them off until you are an intern or a resident. As we indicated earlier, the stakes for you are so high, there is much riding on your becoming a doctor that, by any standard whatsoever, it is a most worthwhile outlay. In every sense of the word, it is an investment in yourself. There are some lending companies which specialize in loans for educational purposes. There are others which pay off your education bills as they come due, while you pay the company or insurance agent in installments over a much longer period of time. Your college or hometown banker is the best source of information about such matters. Hopefully, if you have followed up all of the leads suggested in this section, you can get by without burdening yourself with any loans that are unduly large or long-term.

Other Sources. If you are the offspring of a deceased, disabled, or retired worker covered by Social Security, you may well find that you are entitled to benefits toward you educational expenses until you are 22 years old. If you are a veteran or the wife, widow, widower, or child of a veteran who died or became permanently and totally disabled as a result of military service, you may be qualified to receive regular aid toward you college expenses. You should check on your eligibility for such benefits with the nearest Social Security or VA office while you are still busy making up your list of possible income sources.

CHAPTER 5

GETTING STARTED

You must always envision your career as a continuum, beginning with high school and lasting until your retirement. You must regard that first job or assignment which comes directly after you complete your residency as extremely important. In order to select your first position as carefully and logically as possible, it is wise to make a check list of considerations to be taken into account. More or less in chronological order, the following check list should be suggestive. Of course, you may wish to omit some items and add others in order to bring the whole thing completely into line with your own special needs and preferences.

1) Decide on a specialty.
2) Consider alternatives to the usual career start.
3) Work out a timetable.
4) Determine the kind of affiliation and organizational alliance you are best suited for.
5) Select the type of practice you prefer.
6) Decide on the geographical location and kind of community you prefer.
7) Decide on the image you wish to project.
8) Join appropriate organizations.
9) Subscribe to professional journals and newsletters and inspect everything that might be helpful in your job quest.
10) Spread the word about your interest in a job.
11) Register with your school's placement office.

12) Arrange for references.
13) Obtain transcripts, copies of licenses, certificates, etc.
14) Organize for the job-hunt.
15) Prepare your resume.
16) Draft your letter of application.
17) Register with commercial placement agencies.
18) Prepare for interviews.

Decide on a specialty. Presumably, during your years as a medical student, intern, or resident you will have found one or more areas of psychiatry particularly appealing. These may be broad or they may be comparatively narrow—for example, general psychiatry, which is a broad area, as opposed to child neurology, which is specialized; or perhaps psychoanalysis in contrast to the specific area focusing on psychiatric aspects of gynecological disorders. Even after all your experience, you may be torn between two or more specialties. The 1970 APA poll indicated that many psychiatrists divide themselves between various settings, assignments, and, often, widely diverse problems. If you cannot make up your mind about one particular concentration, it is often possible to arrange for more than one affiliation or job.

In any case, you are strongly advised to settle either on one or on several specialties. Even if you decide not to start your practice immediately, such a decision cannot be postponed. All courses you elect and all jobs or appointments you seek should, in one way or another, enrich the preparation for your special interests.

Consider alternatives. Early in your professional life, you must give consideration to all of the career alternatives which are open to you. The following are a few of the paths you might choose:

• Postgraduate study in such fields as community psychiatry or public health.

• Research in a field relating to your specialty, perhaps assisting at your medical school or at the institution where you completed your residency requirements.

• Public service work in an urban setting or in a depressed rural area like Appalachia, on an Indian reservation, or in a foreign country.

• Volunteer work for a U.S. overseas aid project.

• A tour of duty in one of the armed services.

• U.S. Public Health work as a commissioned officer.

Work out a timetable. If you are planning an active job search, set for yourself a firm schedule, basing it on leave periods during your residency or at its conclusion. In order to be efficient and effective, you must set deadlines for yourself on when you will start and conclude the various phases of job hunting.

Determine the kind of affiliation and organizational alliance you are best suited for. Now the time has come for you to make decisions which will determine the course and nature of both your professional and personal life for the next 30-40 years. Only you can make the necessary determination as to the kind of mental health facility with which you wish to affiliate—or whether, in fact, you do wish to form such an affiliation. Some practitioners prefer to have only the most loose kind of alliance with a facility; others choose either a part- or full-time contractual relationship. If you wish to have patients referred to you or to have an entree for your own patients, it is desirable to form an affiliation with one or more local facilities. The Public Health Service uses the following breakdown of affiliations and organizations:

• Psychiatric hospital—state, county, or proprietary

• VA hospital

• General hospital with psychiatric inpatient and/or out-patient services

• General hospital outpatient psychiatric services

- Residential treatment center for emotionally disturbed children
- Federally funded community health center
- Day hospital
- Other multi-service facilities

In addition, there are the major locations used by the APA in its report on the 1970 poll:

- State mental hospital
- General hospital
- Community mental health center
- Medical school
- Government health or mental health administration agency
- Private mental hospital
- Institute or school for mentally retarded and/or emotionally disturbed
- Correctional institution or prison
- Health or mental health association or foundation
- Drug addiction and rehabilitation center
- College, university, elementary or secondary school or school system
- Alcoholism center
- Nursing home

Select the type of practice you prefer. The latest available study at this writing shows that there are over 6,000 group practices of three or more physicians, with half being single specialty groups, the usual pattern for any group including psychiatrists. Increasingly, because of financial advantages, high income physicians have tended to incorporate their practices rather than form partnerships or become self-employed.

Choose the geographical location and kind of community. Geographical location is, indeed, important to your happiness. It is well to remember that the best financial or professional opportunities may be found in locations with which you are not now familiar. Therefore, don't box yourself in if a particularly attractive appointment or job happens to come along in an area with which you are not familiar. Take stock of your interests and hobbies, investigate the proposed community carefully, then decide if the area offers the kind of lifestyle—private and professional—you prefer.

Decide on the image you wish to project. It is never too early to think about the image you show to the world. Some time ago, while I was serving as a consultant for a medical university, one of the deans angrily expressed to me his outrage over a medical student's careless appearance. It seemed to me that the student was subtly indicating his less than enthusiastic approval of the Establishment by his appearance. The dean, who strongly identified with the status quo, was reacting completely in character. In the long run, of course, the student was not only hurting himself in his current role but also his chances of achieving a choice residency or internship. Moreoever, it is not too early to begin to think about the impression you might be making on people you will ask to serve as your references. Even while you are a student, you should so conduct yourself that they can visualize you as the future doctor in independent practice, moving easily in the various settings required by your responsibilities.

Furthermore, inasmuch as you will be going out on interviews for future jobs or assignments, you should be thinking of your appearance at such times. Be sure you hair is well-groomed and your clothes presentable. Job interviews are so important that it would be well, particularly if you don't have many clothes, to put aside your "interview outfit," having it ready to wear at interview time. Make certain your clothes are clean, well-pressed, and that all of the buttons, belt loops, cuff-links, and the rest are in good condition and ready to wear.

Join appropriate organizations. If you haven't already done so, you should not delay in joining all of the appropriate organizations. It is imperative, of course, to apply for member-in-training with the APA after the first year of approved psychiatric residency. And, of course, after completion of an approved residency, you should immediately apply for general membership in the APA. After five years as a general member, if you have made significant contributions to the field, your district branch may nominate you for Fellowship. Additionally, you should join all of the other organizations in your specialty and some in medicine as a whole.

Frequently, new organizations for sub-specialties of psychiatry emerge. It is often helpful in the early stages of your career to affiliate yourself with one or more of these and use them as a vehicle to promote visibility. Initially, such groups often are desperate for help with organizational matters, subscriptions, journal articles, or speeches, and they welcome those who offer help.

Subscribe to professional journals and newsletters and inspect everything that might be helpful in your job quest. As a member of a professional organization, you will receive some journals, newsletters, and the like, but there will also be some publications that you should subscribe to directly in order to keep current in your specialty.

Spread the word about your interest in a job. As you seek a permanent job, do not be reluctant to speak to others about your quest. Ask the doctors and administrators with whom you come in contact during the course of your work as a resident. They may have useful suggestions which you can follow up. You may be offered positions at the center where you are completing your residency or within the community or area. This may suit you perfectly, in which case no further searching will be necessary. But be certain before you commit yourself that you have at least examined some other possibilities. People like to be asked for help and advice. By talking to some of the professionals in your orbit, you may find yourself developing a rapport with them which will enable you to use them as references later on.

Register with your placement office or its equivalent. Both your medical school and your undergraduate college probably have placement offices which help graduates locate jobs. For you, the principal function of the placement office may not be to inform you about possible vacancies for which you are qualified but rather, to act as a depository for your transcript and other records and original copies of your letters of recommendation. Upon request, they will send these out to persons with a legitimate reason for wanting to study your background.

It behooves you, therefore, well before you are seeking a post-residency job, to register with your placement office and to obtain its instruction sheet. You may have to pay a fee. Often it is a small, lifetime assessment; at other times, there is no fee for your first job. They probably will give you blanks for use by those who will write references for you, to be returned directly to the placement office. Additionally, placement offices, particularly the very specialized ones like those at medical schools, often have files and bulletin boards with announcements of jobs, new programs, and other information of value to the job-hunter.

Arrange for references. During the early phases of your career, as an intern, resident, or seeker of that "first job," it is essential to arrange for references. References are useful to a prospective employer or screening committee because they give insights into the sort of person you are by responsible individuals who have worked with you or seen how you perform. There is no point in obtaining a reference from a person whose knowledge of you is slight, or non-professional, such as someone who has known you only in the capacity of athlete or bridge player, or from one who is not going to say complimentary things about you.

Unless the person you ask for a reference has secretarial help, stationery, and postage for all non-personal business, you should

Special consideration should be given to the various specialty areas and career paths available to psychiatrists.

offer to assist in paying for these items. Don't ask the people you have selected as references to write one letter after another. Either save up several requests and ask for them all at one time or, and this is by far the best procedure, ask that the reference be sent to your placement office. That way, the written document of the reference will always be available for photocopying and mailing.

Remember that it is never appropriate for you to see a written reference about yourself. References should always be sent directly to prospective employers, placement offices, or employment agencies by mail from the person writing the reference. In fact, it is polite (and efficient) for you to supply a stamped, addressed envelope for its transmission.

Obtain transcripts, copies of licenses, certificates, etc. It is extremely important that you have complete records of your academic career, examination results, certificates, and the like, both in your personal files and at the placement office you will use. Whenever possible, you should have the originals in your own possession and never let go of them. If proof of their existence is needed for prospective employers, either have copies made or pay to have duplicates of the originals made by the issuer. Sometimes, you will have to go back to the original issuer because those wishing copies must have them with the originator's embossed seals or signatures. Unfortunately, the use of copying machines has led to a certain amount of document forgery. To offset this, some organizations have been forced into a policy of either insisting on copies with the official embossed seal or other authorization or at least having it come in the mail with a cover letter from the point of origin. Do not be disturbed by such a stipulation. In the long run, it protects you.

It is important to keep in mind that a date, a name, or an address which may seem clear and vivid to you now can be forgotten or slightly garbled with the passage of time. To prevent errors, you should record all pertinent personal career facts and file them in a secure place without delay.

Organize for the job-hunt. The job-hunt is an important matter for you. Everything you do in connection with it is critical to you professionally. Preparations are important, and you should go about them methodically. If you cannot set aside one location to use as a work center, at least arrange to have everything you need in one place—in files, envelopes, or boxes. Buy good typewriter paper, business style envelopes, a package of carbon paper, stamps, several new ballpoint pens, a new ribbon for your typewriter, erasers, and a copy of the latest *Mental Health Directory* (available from the National Institute of Mental Health). The *Directory* gives you hundreds of addresses of clinics and hospitals all over the country, as well as a list of pertinent mental health-related organizations in categories covering a gamut of fields from aging and autism to testing and welfare. If you still haven't joined the APA, you should order copies of several of the most recent issues of *Psychiatric News* or else go to a library and make photocopies of the four or five pages of classified notices of job vacancies found in each issue of this official biweekly newspaper.

There are some obvious points to consider in your organization and procedure:

• Be efficient and businesslike. Keep carbons of all letters written. Make lists of correspondence, if and when replies are received, and a note as to what action by you, if any, is required.

• Make your letters attractive. Be sure your typewriter keys are clean and your ribbon is a new one.

• Set a minimum number of letters which you will write per week and force yourself to meet this number.

• If you don't hear from a prospective employer within two weeks, write again, or try telephoning.

• Acknowledge all letters, even those which are rejections.

• Don't permit yourself to become discouraged. If something seems to be going wrong, try to determine if the fault may lie with you. At all times, be objective and analytic. If there is an older person who might be helpful or an unofficial medical sponsor of some kind, try to get a second opinion. Perhaps you are making some simple error in judgment or in your approach. Perhaps you are not being realistic about what the employers want or what you have to offer them.

• Do not relax for a minute. Frequently, individuals and organizations approached about a job may give you the impression they are more interested in you than is actually the case. For example, they may imply that you are their only candidate, that you'll be hearing from them in short order, that the decision will be made as soon as there has been a meeting or consultation. Don't be lulled into inactivity on the strength of such comments; such phraseology all too frequently is merely a polite way of saying no. Keep plugging away on yet another job possibility until you have signed an agreement to assume a new position.

Otherwise, you may find that a vacancy for which you were fully qualified has been given to some other person with fewer qualifications but more persistence.

Prepare your resume. Some syndicated columnists and self-styled management consultants who write glibly on jobs and careers tend to play down the value and utility of resumes. As a veteran of many hundreds of interviews, from both sides of the desk, I can state that actually your resume, whether mailed along with your letter or taken by you to an interview, is the single most valuable job-landing invention ever devised. It is a short, vivid biography of you which gives the reader an immediate understanding of the important factors in your life. In the clearest, most effortless way, a resume presents all the basic information needed. With this in front of the interviewer, it is possible to plunge right into the essence of the discussion—your long-range career objectives, distinctive capabilities, special interests and hobbies, and so forth.

A resume is a dispassionate, factual, essentially chronological account of your life. It supplements a letter or an interview so that prospective employers and interviewers can move ahead from a point of prior knowledge about you. There is no preferred format, although in your case, since you are in the early stages of your career, it would be desirable to have it fit on one typewritten page. An extremely detailed summary which might supplement the basic resume might include such matters as research projects in which you had participated and articles or books you had written or co-authored.

A resume can often be focused on the kind of job for which you are applying, even though your career is just beginning. For example, if you are being considered for a job on an Indian reservation, you could mention any pertinent experience you may have had in this area. Similarly, if you are hoping for a job with autistic children, it would be helpful to mention that your attention was first directed to this field because you had a younger brother or sister so afflicted. If you are applying for a position in a student health office, neither of these bits of information would be particularly useful and would only clutter up your resume.

The resume should be identified as being yours at the top, with your full name. Other items in essentially the following sequences are:

- Address and telephone number
- Career objectives
- Educational background
- Work experience (in reverse order, last employment first), giving job titles and, if pertinent to a mental health career, some job descriptions as well
- Special interests or hobbies
- Personal data, (age, sex, marital status, social security number, place of birth or nationality)
- Any other information of interest, for example, military background, awards, publications, etc.
- Names, titles, affiliations, addresses, and telephone numbers of your three or four references

Each resume should be either an original or a legible photocopy. Never use a carbon copy or a resume which is not neat and error-free.

Draft your letter of application. Letters of application should always go to a specific person or to an appropriate position or office, for example, "Chief of Staff, Cable Hospital." If you are replying to an advertisement, perhaps one in the *Journal of the American Medical Association* or *Psychiatric News,* be certain to conform precisely to the name and/or title given in the notice.

Take pains with the letter; like an ambassador, it is your representative. Because it will be scrutinized carefully and critically, it should reflect you at your best. You should write as warmly as you can, even though it is to a stranger, indicating that you have something of real value to him and his organization. The letter should be written with great care and should not appear self-centered. Obviously, it should not contain any grammatical errors or be unclear. You should refrain from repeating tired words or phrases. As you write the first draft, you will likely be too worried about making an error to do a really first-rate job; so make a rough draft and then lay it aside overnight. The next day, you may notice an error or an ambiguity which slipped past you when you first wrote it. Don't ever copy a suggested letter out of a book or magazine article. Be yourself and be original. Send a copy of the resume with the letter. Ask for an interview. End the letter by indicating when you are available for an interview and asking the recipient to specify a time. Do not mention salary or travel expenses in the first letter. Give the appearance of seriousness but avoid anything that smacks of self-pity or your "right" to an interview or job. If you don't receive a reply in two weeks, write another, similar letter, referring to your previous correspondence and enclosing another resume.

Register with commercial placement agencies. You will find that in the final analysis, you will locate jobs because of your own efforts and because of a better-than-average performance on your previous assignments. While at times you may feel almost swamped with job offers, at other times, there will be a real or imagined scarcity. As stated above, right from the beginning it is best to employ all the placement offices which are available to you in your job hunt—those of your alma mater, your medical school, and the institution where you did your internship or residency.

However, there are additional sources of help. The local and regional offices affiliated with state and federal employment services are remarkably good. They often have listings of vacancies or other useful information. Immediately before and after medical and public health conferences held in their areas, they are usually particularly well-supplied with job descriptions, information about new programs, and the like.

If all else fails, don't hesitate to seek out a well-recommended commercial employment agency. Some of the better ones which advertise in medical journals and other professional society publications can be extremely helpful. However, in view of your specialized and costly education, you should be very selective about which agency you choose. Select one recommended by those whose opinion you value. While it is true that the commercial agencies charge you a fee, they may lead you to a vacancy which you might not otherwise have found. In some instances, the employer pays the agency fee; however, no matter who pays it, the fee is agreed upon in advance and usually is not out of line, considering the help you receive.

Prepare for interviews. As we discussed previously in association with medical school admissions interviews, you should have your complete wardrobe for the interview ready and waiting. Job interviews are very important, but don't be overly nervous about them. If you are well prepared, they should go smoothly. Try to look your best by grooming carefully and by getting plenty of rest the night before the interview. Be on time. If the appointment is out-of-town, arrive the day before at your lodgings. Promptness is important, so leave yourself plenty of time to find the office. If time permits, you may want to locate the interview site well in advance to avoid the possibility of being tardy because you were lost.

Plan to arrive five minutes early. Do not have anything with you except a copy of your resume and a small pad on which to take notes. Get rid of your outer garments and the like as soon as possible, preferably in the reception room. If you have luggage, leave it in your car, at the airport, or in your hotel. After the greeting, thank the interviewer for seeing you and then let him or her carry the conversational ball.

Use the interview as a learning experience. Ask questions which pertain directly to the job; refrain from asking about trivial matters at the first meeting, such as questions about the local climate or sports facilities. On the other hand, there would be nothing wrong in your inquiring about the housing situation and, if you have children, about the local schools. Questions about the organization, its history, and its likely future would all be appropriate. Keep your eyes and ears open in order to obtain insights into the organization's customs, environment, and morale. Do people use first names? Are the halls and stairwells clean? If it is a school whose accreditation is uncertain, what is its current status? Do your prospective colleagues seem to be current on the latest mental health approaches? Do they have any federal grants? Is there a long-range building and expansion program?

When the interview seems to be approaching its natural conclusion, stand up, express thanks for the time and attention extended to you, collect your possessions, and leave reasonably quickly, after making certain that you aren't leaving anything behind you! It is not inappropriate to ask if and when you will hear from the interviewer, but you may feel it will be better to take care of this in correspondence. Don't appear too eager; however, if you would like to be considered seriously for the position, say so. Remember, you are already in the top group of candidates or they wouldn't have invited you for an interview.

When you return home, send a thank-you letter at once, supplying any extra information the interviewer may have requested and telling him how much you would like to be given serious consideration for the vacancy. Never invent an imaginary need to know their decision promptly. Organizations are extremely cautious about committing themselves, and if they were pressed in such a manner, their most likely response would be to give you a prompt answer in the negative, rather than ask you to wait.

Having completed the interview process, it is now time for you to begin considering other positions. Days, weeks, or even months may elapse before a decision will be made by the employer, and you should continue to investigate other positions until you hear something definite. Continue writing letters and arranging for additional job interviews. Don't stop searching until you have a definite promise of employment.

CHAPTER 6

EMPLOYMENT AND SALARIES
OF PSYCHIATRISTS

For some time to come, the general shortage and imbalanced distribution of psychiatrists and other mental health personnel in the U.S. will contribute to a persistent demand for psychiatrists. For that reason, it should continue to be relatively easy for well qualified psychiatrists to find employment in the locations and specialties they desire.

In this chapter, we will examine employment of psychiatrists in terms of type of work, geographic distribution (including the topic of urban versus rural work), places of work, outlook for the future, and salaries.

TYPE OF WORK

A 1970 poll by the American Psychiatric Association revealed information about members' areas of psychiatric specialization. The survey listed fourteen general subfields and allowed space to write in others. With 2.5 percent subsumed under "other," the rest were distributed as follows:

General psychiatry	48.3%
Adult psychiatry	12.9%
Psychoanalysis	10.5%

Child psychiatry	9.3%
Administrative psychiatry	6.2%
Community or social psychiatry	4.2%
Adolescent or student mental health	2.3%
Forensic psychiatry	1.0%
Neuropsychiatric science	1.0%
Geriatric psychiatry	0.5%
Correctional psychiatry	0.4%
Mental retardation	0.4%
Industrial psychiatry	0.1%

GEOGRAPHIC DISTRIBUTION

When the 1970 APA poll examined geographic distribution, the overall national ratio of psychiatrists was approximately one per 7,995 persons. Other data indicated that in one-half of the states, there were seven or fewer psychiatrists per 100,000 population. When you compare the percentage of the total population in each state and the percentage of the national psychiatric manpower, you find that 54.2 percent of the U.S. population and 66 percent of the psychiatrists are concentrated in ten states (California, Florida, Illinois, Massachusetts, Michigan, New Jersey, New York, Ohio, Pennsylvania, and Texas). At the opposite end of the scale, ten states account for 18.3 percent of the population but possess only 9.5 percent of the psychiatrists. Two states, California and New York, had 9.7 percent and 8.9 percent of the population, respectively, but possessed 13.9 percent and 20.3 percent respectively of the psychiatrists. Most of the states, of course, had comparable extremes within their borders when you consider economically depressed inner city and rural areas as opposed to affluent urban and suburban sections.

The rank order of states according to the ratio of psychiatrists to population is of interest insofar as selecting a location for residency or practice is concerned. There are advantages in selecting an area with fewer psychiatrists but there also are obvious opportunities in areas which have many psychiatrists. The rank order is as follows: District of Columbia, New York, Maryland, Massachusetts, Connecticut, California, Colorado, Vermont, Kansas, Pennsylvania, Rhode Island, Missouri, Delaware, Hawaii, Washington, New Hampshire, New Jersey, Illinois, Michigan, Virginia, Florida, Wisconsin, Ohio, Oregon, Arizona, Texas, Louisiana, North Carolina, Georgia, Utah, Iowa, Minnesota, Nebraska, New Mexico, Alaska, Maine, Arkansas, Oklahoma, Kentucky, Tennessee, Puerto Rico, Nevada, South Carolina, Indiana, North Dakota, South Dakota, Mississippi, Montana, Alabama, West Virginia, Wyoming, Idaho.

For a long time to come, the majority of hospital beds designated for psychiatric patients will be predominantly along the eastern seaboard and in California; but South Dakota, Wisconsin, and Wyoming also rank high. Finances, traditional attitudes toward mental illness, size, population density, and general inertia seem to explain the low numbers which characterize other states. The important factor to keep in mind is that all states have *some* mental hospital beds. When you consider the impact of the new drugs and techniques on the whole mental health field, perhaps those states without large numbers of beds may find it easier to forge ahead than will some of those already possessing large psychiatric hospital facilities. Those which currently lag behind may move aggressively into the community-oriented programs which seem to be the wave of the future. Considering that possibility, it may be that the distribution of psychiatrists will be more important than the number of hospital beds. You will, however, want to weigh both factors when deliberating your decision about where to locate.

PLACES OF WORK

Having discussed the geographic distribution of psychiatrists, let us now turn to their specific job settings—the kinds of institutions or organizations in which they serve. The 1970 American Psychiatric Association poll studies in some detail the professional activities of psychiatrists. The most striking revelation was the considerable amount of independence they enjoyed. Fewer than 39 percent of psychiatrists limit their activities to one setting; the most common pattern is for them to operate in two or more settings involving many types of activities. They may, for example, combine private practice with several institutional affiliations. The listing below gives, in order of frequency, the settings in which the respondents to the APA poll were working:

> Private office
> General hospital
> State mental hospital
> Medical school
> Community mental health center
> Government health or mental health
>   administration agency
> Private mental hospital
> University
> Institution or school for mental retardation
>   and/or emotionally disturbed
> Correctional institution or prison
> Elementary school system
> Other institutions of higher education
> Mental health (or health) association
>   or foundation
> College
> Drug addiction and rehabilitation center

Nursing home
Secondary school system
Alcoholism center

Within these settings, the respondents spent their work hours in the following activities, in order of frequency:

Direct patient contact
Consultation
Teaching
Research
Administration

URBAN VERSUS RURAL WORK

The shortage of psychiatrists in urban areas is well known to all of us. However, all of our large cities have hospital emergency rooms or mental health facilities within comparatively easy reach, even though they may be understaffed. The shortage of psychiatrists actually is more acute in rural areas. If country living appeals to you, establishing a rural practice or finding a salaried job should be relatively easy.

The individual states have the responsibiliy for the care of their mentally ill and retarded; consequently, the standards of care differ widely. In our most rural states, the ratio of psychiatric beds per 1,000 population is only one-tenth that of the four most urban states (New York, California, Pennsylvania, and Massachusetts).

In rural areas, the lack of adequate mental health facilities often leads to shockingly inappropriate treatment of those who need psychiatric services. Alcoholics, juvenile delinquents, abandoned children, and people who are merely confused or actually psychotic frequently are tossed into local jails. While the more affluent rural residents often can and do seek health care in distant cities, both money and transportation are serious problems for the rural poor.

NIMH programs have endeavored to correct the critical rural shortages and problems. During the period 1948-73, it provided financial support for the training of more than 48,000 people in the four core mental health disciplines of psychiatry, psychology, social work, and nursing. In addition, medical school programs in psychiatry reached approximately 25,000 students. NIMH has also supported a wide variety of other endeavors designed to improve the skills of mental health professionals and nonprofessionals working in rural areas, and to provide training in mental health principles and practices to clergymen, teachers, and others who might have substantial influence on the community's welfare. Despite these efforts, rural shortages are still great and the demand for psychiatrists continues to mount.

If you should have some definite interest in rural practice, you would be well advised to take advantage of some of the NIMH programs specifically designed to introduce students to the special needs of rural areas. One of these is part of the child psychiatry program at the University of Kentucky. Yale University also has programs for undergraduates which offer the opportunity to gain clinical experience by serving with mental health teams working in rural settings.

SPECIAL COMMUNITY WORK

Because so many of today's medical students are concerned with helping to make our nation a better place in which to live,

Employment opportunities and salary ranges are determined by the specialty and geographic area in which you choose to work.

they contemplate serving in a less than affluent community; to become involved in it; and to assist in the delivery of psychiatric and other mental health services to help who otherwise might be denied them. The NIMH has been extremely successful in supporting significant community psychiatry components in basic residency programs as well as in the more advanced training of specialists for such activity. Throughout, the aim has been to give the psychiatrist greater knowledge of the diverse socio-environmental factors which influence individual personality and behavior.

OUTLOOK FOR THE FUTURE

Thanks to the imagination, industry, and research of psychiatrists, both in and outside NIMH, an extremely broad spectrum of mental health approaches to individual and social problems has developed. But many programs are held up for want of psychiatric leadership. Hundreds of communities are desperate for the services of a psychiatrist behind whom they can rally.

In view of the current critical shortages and growing awareness of the value of psychiatry, it is unlikely that there will be heavy competition for jobs in coming years. There will be a continuing need to replace annually a large number of doctors who die, retire, or move into positions which involve no patient care whatsoever. In addition, more and more physicians are reducing the number of hours they work a week, and some elderly doctors are refusing to accept new patients. Their reduced patient loads require that other psychiatrists set up practices or increase the number of patients they treat.

Certain demographic factors can be counted upon to increase the demands upon the available doctor supply, including:

- Population growth
- Declining death rate
- Growing numbers of new patients created by newly extended pre-payment programs for hospitalization and medical care, including Medicare and Medicaid
- The continued provision by the federal government of medical care for members of the armed forces, their families, and veterans
- The increasing use of doctors for positions involving administrative, research, teaching, public health, rehabilitation, and industrial medicine

Whatever your preferences, the continuing shortage of psychiatrists makes it likely that when you have completed your training, you should be able to handpick your residential location, professional affiliation, and specialty.

SALARIES

For most psychiatrists, the financial rewards of the profession are extremely satisfying. In view of their long professional education and the large financial investment it requires, it would seem logical for psychiatrists to expect to earn above average salaries and fees.

According to *Medical Economics,* a journal which concentrates on the financial and other non-medical aspects of physicians' lives, the median annual income of psychiatrists is $43,354. (Median is the point at which half the figures are greater and half are smaller.) Looking at the total picture, psychiatrists' earnings break down as follows:

$80,000 or more	7%
$70,000-79,999	5%
$60,000-69,999	7%
$50,000-59,999	17%
$40,000-49,999	20%
$30,000-39,999	21%
Below $30,000	23%

From these figures, you can see that even those psychiatrists on the bottom rung of the income ladder earn good livings. The following employment advertisements, selected at random from newspapers and professional journals, will give an indication of the salaries of typical positions available to psychiatrists:

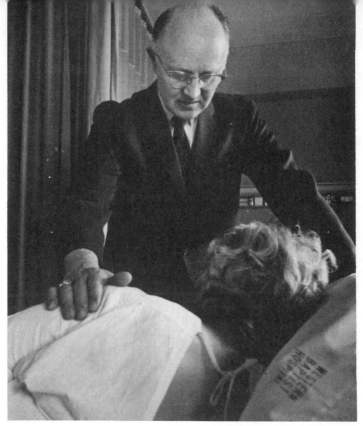

Psychiatrists may work in urban or rural environments and in hospital, office, or community settings.

PSYCHIATRIST

To work in service center in Puerto Rico neighborhood. Must have state license and drug program experience; half-time position. Salary $15,825

PSYCHIATRISTS

Several needed for small psychiatric hospital. Must have completed residency and hold state licensure. Liberal fringe benefits. Salary: $26,654 to $28,786 with yearly increases.

PSYCHIATRIST

University-affiliated community mental health facility requires psychiatrist with state license and three years of residency. Salary: $28,141-$35,573

PSYCHIATRIST

Work in large private hospital; free house and opportunity for private patients; must have state license. Salary: $32,500 to $38,000.

DIRECTOR

For comprehensive mental health center. Must be board-certified psychiatrist. Similar experience important. Salary: Up to $50,000

PSYCHIATRIST

Faculty position, medical college. Salary: $30,000 to $49,000.

SALARIES OF RESIDENTS

This chapter would be incomplete without a discussion of the salaries paid to psychiatric residents. Past generations of doctors often endured residencies when long—almost inhumane—hours of work with patients were compounded by salaries which made even basic comforts virtually unattainable and the support of dependents difficult, if not out of the question. Those days are gone forever, although long hours of work and periods of "on call" often create great fatigue and emotional exhaustion. Actually, in some of the large cities, many residents somehow manage to make private "house calls" for doctors who have their own practices, so the drain on energies and skills of residency seems to be within the limits of human toleration, if only by a small margin. Today's residents receive salaries which make possible lives of dignity and comfort, if not luxury, and the decent support of dependents. In addition, there are frequent fringe benefits in the way of housing, meals, laundry, allowances for dependents, and the like. By and large, residencies pay the most to those with state licenses and completed internships.

According to the American Psychiatric Association's *A Descriptive Directory of Psychiatric Training Programs in the United States,* salaries for first-year resident psychiatrists in 1973 generally ranged from under $9,000 to more than $17,000. Second year residencies ranged from under $11,000 up to almost $18,000. For the third year, the resident can expect to receive from under $12,000 up to $20,000, although most were in the high teens. One five-year plan had the following stipends:

$14,600; $16,900; $19,700; $24,700; and $26,100. Another five-year program paid $16,500 for each of the first three years, which were followed by two "on the staff" at $21,800 and $23,700. Depending on the institution's location, financial condition, affiliation, and a host of other factors, the stipends vary tremendously. You must weigh the value to you of the programs and location, along with a candid appraisal of your own worth as you decide to which institutions you will apply. It is important to keep firmly in mind as you seek out your residency appointment that the value of the program and experience to you, your own special interests, and your career plans are vastly more important than the salary, the location, and such matters as housing, recreational facilities, and the like. Remember that you are being paid to undergo an exciting and intellectually rewarding period of professional training for which many others would pay to be permitted to experience themselves.

CHAPTER 7

PROFESSIONAL ACCREDITATION

In terms of education, public scrutiny, external controls, and the judgement of one's peers, it is very difficult to become and remain a psychiatrist. The screening process begins with the Medical College Admission Assessment Program which is taken during the undergraduate years and continues throughout the psychiatrist's professional life. Medical school, internship, and residency are only the beginning. The psychiatrist must also face licensing, certification, and professional acceptance by one of several organizations.

LICENSING

Passing of the "boards" (an examination administered by the National Board of Medical Examiners, part of which may be taken during medical school) qualifies the psychiatrist for practice in most states. Furthermore, while still a medical student, it is usually advisable to take the examinations set by state authorities where you plan to practice. Moreover, many states accept the National Board of Medical Examiner's certification of a student instead of their state examinations. Because states differ in their licensing requirements and change their regulations frequently, you should look into the prevailing situation in the states where you plan to do your internship or your residency—or eventually to practice. Your salary as a resident is often larger if you have a state license, so you should waste no time in communicating with the office in the state capital concerned with professional certification and credentials evaluation.

CERTIFICATION

Certification is handled by the American Board of Psychiatry and Neurology, Inc., founded in 1934 to assess the competence of specialists in psychiatry and neurology and to certify applicants who were found, upon voluntary examination, to be fully qualified specialists. Currently, in order to be examined for certification in psychiatry, a licensed physician is required to have satisfactorily completed three years of specialized residency training in addition to having two years of experience. In Canada, the Royal College of Physicians and Surgeons of Canada certifies Canadian psychiatrists with requirements similar to those in the United States.

PROFESSIONAL ORGANIZATIONS

Patients, colleagues, and employers have a legitimate interest in your education, memberships, and activities in connection with the APA and other appropriate county, state, regional, and national professional organizations. All of these elements bear on your professional status and hence are important considerations when you are undergoing scrutiny. In large measure this is the case because, as Edgar S. Schein points out in his 1972 *Professional Education,* it is expected that you, as a professional, will be making decisions on behalf of a client or patient in terms of general principles accepted by the profession. It is assumed that you possess a specialized body of knowledge acquired during your regulated and accredited educational experience and that you have passed different examinations and licensing processes. You are presumed to be using your expertise on behalf of the patients' particular needs. The following professional organizations should be of interest to you.

THE AMERICAN PSYCHIATRIC ASSOCIATION

Having considered the various early stages through which you, as a young doctor, must pass and the screening processes you must survive, let us look at the American Psychiatric Association (APA) and its implication for you. The APA is the most important professional organization for prospective or active psychiatrists. You should waste no time in subscribing to its publications and in applying for that category of membership for which you are qualified.

Fellowship is the highest status the Association offers. It is conferred on general members who, over a period of at least five years, have exerted constructive influence in both the Association and their communities. A candidate's ability in clinical work, administration, teaching, or research, along with certification by the American Board of Psychiatry and Neurology, are among the criteria carefully considered before Fellowship is granted.

Member-in-training is a category for those who are in the early stages of their professional career. This status can be retained for no more than five years and may be applied for at the end of the first year of residency. It is wise to make application at the earliest time allowed.

General Members are physicians who have completed at least three years of resident training with either a valid license to practice medicine or employment in a position that does not require licensure. This is the category to which you should aspire after you move up from the member-in-training category.

Associate Members are physicians who have completed at least one year of acceptable training or experience in psychiatry but are not eligible for general membership or member-in-training status. This category might be assigned to those who are primarily in a specialty other than psychiatry.

There are other organizations and associations to which you will wish to belong, including the important and influential American Medical Association whose *Journal* you will wish to read regularly, but the above categories of APA membership are significant milestones in your professional career.

THE AMERICAN BOARD OF
PSYCHIATRY AND NEUROLOGY

Let's now examine the legal and licensing implications of the professional categories conferred by the American Board of Psychiatry and Neurology, mentioned earlier in this chapter.

Board Eligible Psychiatrist refers to a psychiatrist who is eligible to take the examinations of the American Board of Psychiatry and Neurology, usually a doctor who has completed an approved three-year residency training program and two additional years of approved experience in the field.

Board Certified Psychiatrist is a psychiatrist who has taken and passed examinations administered by the American Board of Psychiatry and Neurology and thus becomes certified as a medical specialist in psychiatry. It is impossible to overemphasize the prestige and authority of these credentials. Psychiatrsts who possess them have a substantial advantage over those who do not have them so far as positions, responsibilities, and salary differentials are concerned.

ETHICS AND THE PSYCHIATRIST

Ethics and proper behavior are extremely important matters for all doctors, collectively and individually. The medical profession to which you are aspiring must be so correct and ethical that it should stand above criticism. As a result, it is given by society the privilege of policing itself. Of course, at times, the profession finds this responsibility alternately burdensome and difficult. For example, in February 1976, the South Carolina Medical Association sought from the Legislature a new law to broaden disciplinary action by doctors and their organizations against physicians who were drinking too heavily, taking drugs, or otherwise behaving incompetently. They wanted more power (under state law) to police themselves, apparently fearing a loss of autonomy if they could not perform it more effectively on their own. Members seemed to feel that under the existing laws, they did not have enough "clout" for adequate disciplinary action.

As a group, psychiatrists are particularly vulnerable to charges of malpractice because of the intangible, sensitive nature of much of their work and their patients' illnesses. Unless you can function in hazardous situations, it is not a career for you. Both as a group and as individuals, psychiatrists are subjected to public scrutiny.

Generally the public holds psychiatrists in high regard. There are numerous reasons for this attitude, including the following: a great deal of contributed time by psychiatrists to charity patients and civic causes; recognition of the strenuous, long, and costly preparation required for official status as a psychiatrist; acknowledgment by many intellectuals and professionals in our society that there is considerable thought being given to the ways the psychiatric profession can aid the poor and alienated members of our society.

CHAPTER 8

MINORITY GROUPS AND WOMEN IN PSYCHIATRY

The increasing emphasis on equal educational and employment opportunities for women as well as minority group members is a reflection of the realization that undeveloped talent of any kind is a loss both to the individual concerned and to society at large. In this chapter, we shall examine the impact of this trend on the psychiatric profession.

MINORITY GROUPS

Of all students in U.S. medical schools in 1971-72, 5 percent were black, 0.57 percent were Mexican-American, and 0.08 percent were American Indians. One of every 560 whites becomes a physician, compared with one of every 3,800 blacks. To state it another way, from the 11 percent of the 1970 population which was black came 2.2 percent of the nation's physicians.

The 1970 APA survey of psychiatrists is the latest available. It has tentative but incomplete information on the racial breakdown of the profession. The findings were as follows:

American Indian	0.1%
Black	1.5%
Asian	3.3%
White	94.9%
Other	0.2%

So many Europeans and those from other foreign countries are included that the relationship between native-born U.S. whites and blacks is blurred. It is likely, therefore, that the black-white ratio is much more favorable to blacks than these figures suggest.

The above should be read as a tribute to those minority group members who have surmounted nearly impassable obstacles to advance themselves toward their professional objectives. Additionally, the achievements of these pioneers make it much easier for those who follow them.

Even during periods of economic difficulty, when some assistance programs must be curtailed or cut back, it is becoming increasingly easier for members of minority or disadvantaged groups to advance themselves toward an M.D. degree and a specialty in psychiatry. If yours is a minority background, you should be heartened by the accomplishments of other minority group members, as well as by all the assistance programs available to you. Let's take a quick survey of some of the new programs, procedures, and ways of thinking about members of minority groups who wish to prepare themselves for a career in psychiatry.

SPECIAL PROGRAMS

One of the most successful programs involves making traditional admissions procedures for colleges more flexible and providing more remedial work, counseling, and tutoring than used to be thought necessary. Equally valuable are provisions for giving students academic credit for pertinent work experiences. New Jersey has established Thomas A. Edison College to process credits for job-related activities. New York has its Empire State College, whose Educational Opportunity Program is mentioned below, and State University of New York's Cooperative Assessment of Experimental Learning (CAEL) to find better methods to evaluate knowledge gained outside the classroom. The College

Entrance Examination Board is active in converting employment experiences into college credits. If you feel you have the ability to succeed as a student and have had pertinent, responsible job experiences, you should investigate converting them into college credits, either to use for outright tradeoffs for courses or to enable you to obtain advanced placement.

Other encouraging developments of recent years with which minority students should become familiar include the following:

• An increasing number of colleges which are admitting students on the basis of high school equivalency diplomas.

• New career programs and projects for part-time students. Some courses are actually offered on the premises in places of employment.

• State programs providing partial support of private colleges in recognition of the work they are doing to help deprived black and rural students.

• Colleges providing the equivalent of what used to be private, expensive "cram" courses for students needing them, like Philadelphia's "Learning Laboratory," which has study aids, slide and tape resumes of past class meetings, help with writing and mathematics, classes in which the student can progress as slowly or as fast as desired, and such special elective courses as "Psychology of Self."

• Arrangements like New York's Empire State Educational Opportunity Program (EOP), which prepares carefully selected, high potential students with weak backgrounds for study on college campuses. In this program, priority is given to women and those from minority or disadvantaged backgrounds.

• Such publishing ventures as the magazine, *Discovery,* which is designed to help black students identify themselves "in relation to the society they live in."

Because of the prestige of the National Institute of Mental Health, its establishment in 1970 of the Center for Minority

Group Mental Health Programs is an extremely significant measure which should give encouragement to all those from U.S. minorities with an interest in a career in psychiatry. It was set up to serve as a focal point for Institute activities bearing directly on meeting the mental health needs of minority groups. It serves to introduce minority group perspectives into the design, operation, and evaluation of the Institute's research, training, and service activities. The Center stimulates and supports projects intended to increase the number and improve the skills of minority group members engaged in mental health research and training. High priority is given to projects designed to study minority group lifestyles and value systems and their particular mental health problems; the relationships between minority groups; and the perceptions and behavior of minority groups toward one another and toward the majority population.

The prestigious APA has the following groups which are concentrating on matters of concern to minority individuals: Committee of Black Psychiatrists, Task Force Relating to Research Evaluation of Racism, Task Force on Delivery of Psychiatric Services in Poverty Areas, Task Force on Indian Affairs, and the Task Force on Mental Health of Spanish-speaking People in the United States. These groups stem from and are undergirded by APA studies on minorities.

In its 1973 survey of psychiatric residency training programs, the APA queried hospitals and other organizations concerning the recruitment of minorities, their efforts to promote understanding of minority subcultures, and areas of training contributing to these efforts. Although much remains to be done in connection with modernizing the residency programs in many hospitals, the mere fact that the APA is polling hospitals about such reforms will have a great impact on all program directors to "clean house." On balance, from school on through college and into medical school, the internship and the residency, much is being accomplished. Increasingly, a climate of opinion is developing which will, and before too long, make the old days when there was denial of the rights of women and members of minority and disadvantaged groups seem remote and inconceivable. For further information see the appendices to this book.

FINANCIAL AID

In a previous chapter, we discussed finances for your college and medical school education. Sources of aid which are of particular interest to minority group students are discussed below. Additionally, there are three useful federal booklets which you may wish to consult at a library or purchase from a Government Printing Office outlet. They are:

How to Pay for Your Health Career Education, a Guide for Minority Students (Dept. of Health, Education and Welfare Publication #HRA 7408, 65 cents).

Major Federal Student Assistance Programs Administered by the Office of Education (Subcommittee on Labor and Public Welfare, 30 cents).

How Medical Students Finance Their Education (Bureau of Health Resources Development, Health Resources Administration, U.S. Department of Health, Education and Welfare, Free).

You should also know about *Graduate and Professional School Opportunities for Minority Students,* which lists many programs by fields and how they stand regarding minority students. It also gives information on qualifying examinations and sources of financial aid. (Available from Educational Testing Service, Princeton, New Jersey 08549, $3.00).

If you attended a community college and your grades were outstanding, you should check to see if your name appears in *The Talent Roster of Outstanding Minority Community College Graduates* prepared by the CEEB. This contains the names of almost 1,100 students in which four-year institutions may be interested. If your name appears in this listing, you should make mention of this fact when you are applying to a bachelor's degree-granting institution.

Some of the programs of possible interest to you, if you are from a minority or disadvantaged background or are female, are sponsored by the following:

• *Bureau of Indian Affairs Higher Education Program*—A scholarship and loan program for American Indians and Eskimos in financial need. Applications are made through the Bureau's eleven area offices or reservation-based agency offices having record of the student's tribal affiliation. Program description is available from the latter or from the Higher Education Staff, Central Office, Bureau Higher Education Program, P.O. Box 1788, Albuquerque, New Mexico 87103. This office and many tribal headquarters can provide useful information on loans and grants for higher education. Needy students of American Indian descent studying for health careers who are enrolled in or accepted by an accredited school should write to the Executive Secretary, Indian Health Employees Scholarship Fund, Citizens Building, Room 604, Aberdeen, South Dakota 57401.

• *National Scholarship Service and Fund for Negro Students* —A supplementary scholarship fund for black high school students through junior year of college. Write to Mrs. Jean Boatswain, NSSFNS Application Department, 1776 Broadway, New York, N.Y. 10019.

• For information about fellowships for students studying medicine who are also from minority groups—blacks, American Indians, Mexican-Americans, Mainland Puerto Ricans, and native Hawaiians—write to the Executive Secretary, National Medical Fellowships, Inc., 3935 Elm Street, Downers Grove, Illinois 60515.

• For information about loans for black students studying medicine—maximum amounts are $1,500 per year or $7,000 for entire training sequence—write National Medical Association, Inc., 1108 Church Street, Norfolk, Virginia 23510.

• *Upward Bound* and *Special Services for Disadvantaged*— Federal programs for the disadvantaged which make grants through institutions, agencies, and some non-profit making organizations. Check with your college or medical school or write Division of Work-Study and Special Programs, Office of Student Assistance, Bureau of Postsecondary Education, Office of Education, Washington, D.C. 20202.

WOMEN

In terms of the percentage of women practitioners, psychiatry ranks third among all medical fields (after pediatrics and internal medicine). A 1970 study disclosed that 11.4 percent of the psychiatry profession is female, and the proportion of female psychiatry residents is rising, going from 19.8 percent in 1972 to 22.4 percent in 1974.

Another plus for women is the fact that the same 1970 study of U.S. psychiatrists showed that while 24.9 percent of men have completed more than three years of residency training, 29.5 percent of the women have more than three to their credit. It is a reflection of these women's professional initiative that they have undergone additional special training.

In spite of the unique problems female students sometimes encounter, women complete their psychiatric training as often as men do, and their professional activities closely resemble those of men. The major differences between the professional lives of men and women psychiatrists, according to a 1970 APA survey, seem to be the following:

• Women psychiatrists have a greater variety of personal lifestyles than do men, either managing to devote all of their time to their careers, or combining them with marriage, motherhood, and other outside interests.

- Fewer women than men are Board-certified. This means they cannot command the same salaries nor qualify for as many jobs as Board-certified psychiatrists. Professionally they tend to be less mobile.

- More women than men work part-time, are retired, or are employed other than as psychiatrists.

- Although one-quarter of the women had professional commitments in three or more locations, as a group, women tended to diversify their efforts less than men. Women are employed in greater proportions than men in state mental hospitals, schools, colleges, and universities. They tend to be in salaried positions more often than men.

The women averaged 39 hours of work per week while the men put in an average of 49 hours. For most of the cases reported, men did direct patient contact work for 32 hours in an average week, while women did 25 hours. On the other hand, both sexes devoted about the same number of hours to consultation, teaching, research, administration, and a wide variety of charitable activities.

In keeping with the spirit of enhancing opportunities for women, the American Psychiatric Association, at its 1972 annual meeting, formed a women's caucus and appointed a task force to examine not only the role of women in the specialty but also psychiatry's effect on the lives of all women. In 1974, the APA board of trustees accepted the task force's recommendation that there be a standing Committee on Women, with the following main objectives:

- To define and recommend action to meet women's mental health needs by reassessing the current theory and practices of psychiatry in terms of its congruence with the reality of their lives.

• To promote women psychiatrists' involvement in academic research, administration, and professional organizations, along with the development of methods of increasing their participation and leadership.

• To stimulate and develop theories necessary to the improvement of the first two purposes.

• To provide "support systems" for women colleagues; that is, some kind of equivalent for the women of the friendly, personal relationships with colleagues and men instructors which are enjoyed by many male psychiatrists and students.

Women psychiatrists have made an outstanding contribution to society and the profession and have received recognition for their accomplishments. Even so, female psychiatrists must continue to work hard and to cooperate with each other in order to achieve the additional recognition and the access to professional opportunities that they deserve. Equality is vastly overdue in light of their numbers, skills, and professional achievements.

As this chapter was researched, the APA membership totalled 21,746, of whom only 2,591 were women. It was estimated that some 6,000 non-member psychiatrists, including 400-500 women, brought the total number of psychiatrists in this country up to about 27,500. The total of women psychiatrists, some 3,000, is probably around 11 percent of the group.

In conclusion, what should the woman who is considering a career in psychiatry conclude about the wisdom of taking such a step? Do the advantages outweigh the disadvantages? Will her chances for professional success and personal happiness improve or deteriorate? The 1970 APA survey seems to suggest the following:

• In medical school, as an intern, and as a resident, she will encounter occasional discrimination and some hostility. Inter-sex rivalry among those males born since 1950 is decreasing rapidly and is already minimal among those born since 1960. Additionally, the sheer factor of numbers will offset discrimination increasingly. For example, the National Science Foundation has just reported that in 1965 women received 10 percent of the life science doctorates awarded; by 1974, the percentage was 18.

- As a full-fledged psychiatrist, particularly if she has survived respected internship and residency experiences and is Board-certified, she will find herself in great demand by both prospective employers and patients for many reasons. The shortage of psychiatrists will continue indefinitely, so that female psychiatrists and their skills will be a valued commodity. The prestige of the profession and the number of former patients both will become ever greater as pre-paid health plans make psychiatric treatments possible for continually increasing numbers of the population. The public's preoccupation with, and knowledge of, health in general will increase.

- As a woman and as a female psychiatrist, she will encounter some hostility and discrimination from fellow male students, interns, residents, and other physicians. She will have to work harder than her male colleagues to attain the professional "plums" and the top offices in mental health organizations. As the older men resign, retire, or die, more liberal attitudes toward women will increasingly prevail as a matter of course.

- Equal rights for women psychiatrists will become a reality as public opinion and supportive legislation concerning women's rights continue to evolve. The April, 1976, decision of the New York State Court of Appeals, and other similar decisions, that "in proper circumstances, reverse discrimination is constitutional," will greatly strengthen the ability of admissions committees to increase sharply the proportions of women and minority students they accept.

For information about fellowships for women in their last year of medical school, communicate with the Director, Fellowships Office, American Association of University Women, 2401 Virginia Avenue N.W., Washington, D.C. 20037.

If you are a needy woman pursuing a career in medicine, you may be able to qualify for a loan (for U.S. citizens only) from the American Medical Women's Association, Inc., 1740 Broadway, New York, N.Y. 10019.

CHAPTER 9

THE FUTURE OF PSYCHIATRY

Like most thoughtful observers of the contemporary scene, psychiatrists have two major concerns about the America of the future. On the one hand, they are concerned about private problems, namely, those of individuals and their families. Secondly, they are aware of public problems—those conditions which reflect fundamental weaknesses in the fabric of society itself. In recent years, the relationships between social and private problems have been widely recognized.

In summarizing psychiatry's concerns for the future, as useful a device as any is reference to the 1969 "yardsticks" of the President's Panel on Social Indicators. They continue to be valid warnings that social ills persist which underlie much mental illness and misery. They attest to the pervasiveness of social problems and the importance of continuing to study and explore possibilities for their resolution. They are as follows:

Social Mobility. There is opportunity for the majority of our citizens to improve their relative occupational status through their own efforts. Yet we are far from achieving true equality of opportunity. Economic and social status in our society still depends in a striking way on skin color. Until we can eliminate this barrier to full participation, we will not have been faithful to our historic ideals.

Our physical environment. Pollution, land for recreation, and the prevention of urban sprawl are the key factors in this problem area. We must maintain the environment for ourselves and our descendants, recognizing that the problems are multiple and interrelated.

Income and poverty. Although the distribution of income has remained virtually unchanged for many years, rising income levels have meant that fewer and fewer people have incomes below the poverty level. Yet the opportunity structure is not uniformly open. The risk of indigence is much greater for some than for others. Moreover, the poverty of one generation is likely to be perpetuated in the next. How to redistribute our national plenty on fair and socially appropriate grounds is a baffling puzzle.

Public order and safety. Crime is an index of the nation's health and much, obviously, needs to be done to reduce current crime rates.

Learning, science, and art. Greater support for all of these is indicated.

Participation and alienation. Divisions exist between social classes and other groups which should be a subject of greater concern.

Health and illness. Although health is an important national concern, we lag behind other countries in some respects. As in other areas of life, income and financial situation affect one's access to good health.

In all of the above there is a mental health dimension. Each "yardstick" reflects a psychiatric element, and because of this dimension, each has become an important aspect of psychiatry's concern for the future. Psychiatry's principal thrusts are reflected in the work of the National Institute of Mental Health, authorized by the National Mental Health Act. NIMH's major activities include:

Research. The research findings suggest many useful ideas which should be explored. In the first 25 years of NIMH grants, more than 22,500 awards were made, totalling almost $800 million.

Programs. Particularly successful programs have included education of the community concerning the nature of mental illness and the high likelihood of recovery for most patients; giving neighborhood and community leaders a modern frame of reference about mental illness, e.g., who should be referred to mental health centers and who could be cared for at home; traveling teams, TV programs, and other techniques developed on a local base for mental health care along with good liaison and cooperation with state and regional mental health centers.

Community mental health centers. (CMHC). It is hoped a center (CMHC) will eventually be easily accessible to every rural American. In order to qualify for federal support, each center must provide 24-hour emergency care; short-term hospitalization; partial hospitalization; outpatient care; and programs of consultation and education.

When this book was written, federal grants had been made to 540 centers in all 50 states, Puerto Rico, Guam, and the District of Columbia. The five best-equipped states were the following: California, 45 centers; Pennsylvania, 39; Texas, 26; Kentucky, 22; New York, 22. Although the recession of the mid-1970s slowed down funding and the establishment of new centers, at the end of 1973 there were more than 500 serving almost 80 million rural and urban Americans, or 38 percent of the population. Forty percent were rural centers.

Patient release. Today, even though more people than ever before are entering mental health institutions, a large percentage are being returned to their homes and communities or are being placed in nursing homes or halfway houses. Among the factors making this possible are new treatment methods; new objectives characterized by less preoccupation with a cure and more concentration on ability to function independently in the family and home community; new admission policies which screen patients to determine the kind of treatment which would be most useful for them; increasing availability of community-based programs to reduce hospitalization; expansion of third-party payment for expenses incurred during mental illness which permits many who need mental health care to obtain it in the local community; changing public attitudes toward mental illness and those in need of mental health services.

While treatment programs have expanded and increased in numbers, chronic shortages of qualified professionals to staff them have persisted. What are the factors contributing to the shortage? There are eight of them, all relating to the increased demand for mental health services.

The first factor is *population growth.* The U.S. is growing more populous all the time. Hence, we have more individuals needing mental health care. In 1960, we had a population of 180.6 million; in 1970, 204.8 million; between 1970 and 1975, it increased by 10 million to 215 million. When this chapter was researched, the U.S. population was increasing by one person every 20-21 seconds, or more than 4,000 a day. Even assuming a slower rate of growth than in other periods in our history, 1980 will probably find us with 224 million citizens and 1990, with some 246 million.

The second factor is *changing population characteristics.* We have increasing numbers of people in very old age groups, individuals uniquely subject to mental problems. Moreover, the elderly are more and more aware of their political muscle. As this chapter was written, a group of older Philadelphians held a meeting to protest the threat of higher rates for electricity, actually pledging to vote against incumbent city and state officeholders if their demands were ignored. They emphasized that the 25 million "senior citizens" around the country represented a national group whose voice should be respected. We can be sure that mental health care facilities for the aged will continue to expand for many years to come. Another demographic factor is the *rise of educational and economic levels.* With this rise comes greater recognition of health problems and their care/cure, along with ever-increasing demand for and utilization of mental health services.

The third reason for the mental health care personnel shortage is the *steady increase in the percentage of the population which is covered by some type of health insurance.* Understandably, people are much more likely to avail themselves of needed health care if it is covered by insurance. Additionally, there are more and more federal and community-supported programs and facilities which reach or are available to new patients.

Fourthly, there is *greater delegation of responsibilities* to the mental health team by family doctors, employers, and relatives because of growing awareness not only of the mental health dimension of a great deal of physical illness, but also of incidental personal maladjustments, family friction, and drug- or alcohol-abuse.

The fifth reason is the way in which *new therapeutics and technology* are changing patterns of care/cure, particularly for those who formerly would have been committed to mental hospitals. Recent treatment successes actually create personnel shortages since they increase the need for doctors! In 1955, the state mental health hospital population numbered 560,000; by 1969, it had declined to 248,562, a decrease of 56 percent. However, the decrease meant that a tremendous burden was placed on community centers, half-way houses, and other new mental health facilities and specialists. The total workload of the mental health team was substantially increased with the adoption of these modern, more humane, family- or community-centered techniques. While the high patient turnover rate is, of course, most gratifying, it places heavy demands on the available staff and leads to the use of new kinds of allied health personnel, including indigenous aides and lay people.

The sixth factor, related to the preceding, is the *growing need to augment the ready supply of mental health workers.* Social and economic developments such as a shortened workweek, minimum

Population growth and changing population characteristics are two important factors which have led to a shortage of mental health care personnel.

wage, and overtime regulations lead to larger staffs merely to maintain the existing services. In addition, there is increasing utilization of such new techniques as speech pathology, audiology, group work, and recreation therapy. Greater numbers of staff workers and professionals, in turn, require additional numbers of psychiatrists for supervision and administration.

Factor seven, as the House Committee Report on the 1970 Health Training Act emphasized, is that shortages are stimulated by *"an emerging social concept that health care should be a right and not a privilege."*

Item eight is *the general inefficiency of our overall medical care system,* of which mental health is but one component. Because health care is disorganized, with an almost complete absence of planning or quality controls, to a great extent each doctor acts as he or she sees fit. The prevailing pattern of solo practice resembles the cottage industry of a former day. Many critics suggest that a medical care structure which is vastly less extravagant and inefficient is desperately needed, possibly one which has the organizational and procedural characteristics of big business.

SUMMARY

Psychiatry has many attractions. While preparing for it and then as part of its practice, you will participate in one of the most intellectually stimulating careers. Additionally, at all times, you will derive great personal satisfactions from helping not only those who seek you out for help but also their families, friends, neighbors, and business, professional, or student associates. Because it is health-related and because it aids the mentally ill, psychiatry is highly gratifying and timely. Moreover, because health care is ranked as one of the American public's major concerns, you will have the assurance that there is going to be increasing governmental support for the development of mental health facilities, installations, and education.

If you so wish, you will be in a position to encourage and actively engage in various kinds of long-overdue, constructive social changes. If you seek to make psychiatry a medical specialty of high quality, it is likely that you will play a part in making it ever more responsive to public needs. Along this same line, your professional expertise increasingly will be called upon to respond to the less fortunate in our society.

If you are sufficiently motivated to become a qualified psychiatrist, you will probably have no difficulty in finding a job in the location and specialty which suits your interests, desires, and lifestyle. Perhaps the most rewarding dividend of all will be the insights you gain about yourself as you work amidst your patients.

Because of the work, enthusiasm, and insights of the psychiatrists of yesterday and today, the outlook for mental patients and for you as a prospective psychiatrist is the brightest it has ever been. New kinds of treatments, the growing knowledge of behavior-influencing chemicals, the lessons learned from research and from day-to-day work with patients—all of these and more—suggest a future filled with new discoveries, breakthroughs, innovations, and opportunities.

APPENDIX A

RECOMMENDED READING

General:

Association of American Medical Colleges. *Medical School Admission Requirements.* Washington, D.C.: AAMC, 1976.

American Psychiatric Association. *A Psychiatric Glossary.* Washington, D.C.: APA, 1975.

_____ . "Women in Psychiatry." Extracted from October 1973 issue of *American Journal of Psychiatry.* (Pamphlet)

Becker, E. *Revolution in Psychiatry.* New York: Free Press, 1974.

Benetar, J. *Admissions, Notes from a Woman Psychiatrist.* New York: Charterhouse, 1974.

Caplan, G. *Support Systems and Community Mental Health: Lectures on Concept Development.* New York: Behavioral Publications, 1974.

Chapman, A. H. *It's All Arranged, 15 hours in a Psychiatrist's Life.* New York: Berkley, 1976.

Chesler, P. *Women and Madness.* New York: Doubleday, 1972.

Clark. D. H. *Social Therapy in Psychiatry.* Middlesex: Penguin, 1974.

Crain, W. C. *The Psycho Squad.* New York: Saturday Review Press/Dutton, 1976.

de Vito, R. A., and R. P. Tapley, eds. *A View Into a Modern, State-Operated, Mental Health Facility.* Springfield, Illinois: Thomas, 1975.

Dunham, H. W. *Social Realities and Community Psychiatry*. New York: Behavioral Publications, 1975.

Glasscote, R. M., et al. *The Alternative Services: Their Role in Mental Health, A Field of Free Clinics, Runaway Houses, Counseling Centers, and the Like*. Washington: Information Service of the APA and the NAMH, 1975.

Grinker, R. R. *Psychiatry in Broad Perspective*. New York: Behavioral Publications, 1975.

Henry, W. E., J. H. Sims, and S. L. Spray. *Public and Private Lives of Psychotherapists*. San Francisco: Jossey-Bass, 1975.

Keyes, F. *Your Future in a Mental-Health Career*. New York: Rosen, 1976.

Kiev, A. *Transcultural Psychiatry*. New York: Free Press, 1972.

Kovel, J. *A Complete Guide to Therapy, from Psychoanalysis to Behavior Modification*. New York: Pantheon, 1976.

Kramer, B. M. *Racism and Mental Health*. Pittsburgh: University of Pittsburgh, 1973.

Lidz, T., and M. Edelson, eds. *Training Tomorrow's Psychiatrists*. New Haven, Yale, 1970.

Lieberman, E. J., ed. *Mental Health: The Public Health Challenge*. Washington: American Public Health Association, 1975.

Mahrer, A. R., and L. Pearson, eds. *Creative Developments in Psychotherapy, Vol. 1*. Cleveland: Case-Western Reserve, 1971.

May, R. *Love and Will*. New York: Dell, 1974. (Paperback)

McNeely, H. E., and N. Oberle. *Psychotherapy: The Private and Very Personal Viewpoints of Doctor and Patient*. Chicago: Nelson-Hall, 1972.

Pappworth, M. H. *Passing Medical Examinations*. London: Butterworths, 1975.

Park, C. C., with L. N. Shapiro. *You Are Not Alone, Understanding and Dealing with Mental Illness*. Boston: Atlantic-Little Brown, 1976.

Perucci, R. *Circle of Madness: On Being Insane and Institutionalized In America.* Englewood Cliffs, N.J.: Prentice-Hall, 1974.

Peszke, M. A. *Involuntary Treatment of the Mentally Ill: The Problem of Autonomy.* Springfield, Illinois: Thomas, 1975.

Rosenfeld, A., ed. "The Psychotherapy Jungle, a Guide for the Perplexed," *Saturday Review,* Vol. 3, No. 10 (February 21, 1976), pp. 4-5, 12-32.

Rossi, J. J., and W. J. Filstead. *The Therapeutic Community.* New York: Behavioral Publications, 1973.

Rubin, T. I. *Shrink!* New York: Popular Library, 1974.

_____, with E. Rubin. *Compassion and Self-Hate, an Alternative to Despair.* New York: Ballentine, 1975. (Paperback)

Viscott, D. S. *The Making of a Psychiatrist.* New York: Fawcett, 1973.

Financial Aid:

College Entrance Examination Board, *Meeting College Costs: A Guide for Parents and Students* (CEEB, Box 2815, Princeton, N.J. 08540, Free.

New York Life Insurance Company, *College Costs Today* (Promotion Services, Room 1108, New York Life Insurance Company, 51 Madison Avenue, New York, N.Y. 10010, Free if you send self-addressed, stamped envelope.)

American Medical Association, *Helping Hands* (AMA, 535 North Dearborn Street, Chicago, Illinois 60610, Single copies free from Careers, Department of Health Manpower, AMA, at above.)

U.S. Department of Health, Education, & Welfare (all DHEW publications available from U.S. DHEW, Public Health Service, Health Resources Administration, Washington, D.C. 20201) publications of interest to you:

College Work-Study Program Manual
rev. ed., 1972
Publication No. OE 55045

Entering an Agreement to Practice in a Shortage Area
1973

HEW Fact Sheet
Five Federal Financial Aid Programs
1975
Publication No. OE 75-17907

How Health Professions Students Finance Their Education
Publication No. HRA 74-13

How Medical Students Finance Their Education

*How the Office of Education Assists College Students
   and Colleges*
1970
Publication No. OE 55051-70

*How To Pay for Your Health Career Education
A Guide for Minority Students*
Publication No. HRA 74-8

*Major Federal Student Assistance Programs Administered
   by the Office of Education*
1974
3rd ed.

American Legion, Patterson, R. ed., *Need a Lift? To Educational Opportunities, Careers, Loans, Scholarships, Employment;* Indianapolis, American Legion.

Bureau of Indian Affairs, *Scholarships for American Indians,* Albuquerque, New Mexico.

Chronicle Guidance Publications, *Student Aid Bulletin: Scholarships Offered by Labor Unions.* Moravia, N.Y.: Chronicle Guidance Publications, Inc.

Ebony, Norton, C. A., ed. *The Scholarship Path to a College Degree.* Chicago: Judson Publishing Company, 1975. (Emphasis on needs of black students.)

Johnson, W. L. *Directory of Special Programs for Minority Group Members: Career Information Services, Employment Skills Banks, Financial Aid,* Garrett Park, Maryland: Garrett Park Press, 1974.

National Chicano Health Organization, *Health Careers and Chicanos, 1973-74.* Los Angeles: National Chicano Health Organization.

Navaho Health Authority, *Kellogg American Indian Fellowships, 1975.* Window Rock, Arizona.

APPENDIX B

U.S. MEDICAL SCHOOLS

Alabama
University of Alabama
Birmingham 35294

University of South Alabama
School of Medicine
Mobile 36688

Arizona
University of Arizona School
of Medicine
Tucson 85721

Arkansas
University of Arkansas
School of Medicine
Little Rock 72201

California
Loma Linda University
School of Medicine
Loma Linda 92354

Stanford University
School of Medicine
Stanford 94305

University of California
California College of Medicine
Irvine 92664

University of California (Davis)
School of Medicine
Davis 95616

University of California
at Los Angeles School of
Medicine
Los Angeles 90024

University of California
at San Diego School of
Medicine
La Jolla 92037

University of California
School of Medicine
San Francisco 94122

University of Southern
California School of
Medicine
Los Angeles 90024

Colorado
University of Colorado
School of Medicine
Denver 80202

Connecticut
University of Connecticut
School of Medicine
Farmington 06032

Yale University School of
Medicine
New Haven 06520

District of Columbia
Georgetown University School
of Medicine
Washington 20007

George Washington University
School of Medicine
Washington 20006

Howard University College
of Medicine
Washington 20001

Florida
Program in Medical Sciences
Florida State University
Tallahassee 32306

University of Florida College
of Medicine
Gainesville 32611

University of Miami School
of Medicine
Coral Gables 33124

University of South Florida
(Tampa)
Colleges of Medicine and
Nursing
Tampa 33620

Georgia
Emory University School of
Medicine
Atlanta 30322

Medical College of Georgia
Augusta 30902

Hawaii
University of Hawaii
School of Medicine
Honolulu 96822

Illinois
Chicago Medical School
Chicago

Loyola University
Stritch School of Medicine
Maywood 60611

Northwestern University
Medical School
Chicago 60611

Rush Medical College
Chicago 60612

Southern Illinois University
Springfield 62901

University of Chicago
Pritzker School of Medicine
Chicago 60637

University of Illinois College
of Medicine
Chicago 60680

Indiana
Indiana University School of
Medicine
Indianapolis 46202

Iowa
University of Iowa College
of Medicine
Iowa City 52242

Kansas
University of Kansas School
of Medicine
Lawrence 66045

Kentucky
University of Kentucky
College of Medicine
Lexington 40506

University of Louisville
School of Medicine
Louisville 40208

Louisiana
Louisiana State University
Medical Center (Shreveport)
School of Medicine
Shreveport 71105

Louisiana State University
School of Medicine
New Orleans 70119

Tulane University School of
Medicine
New Orleans 70118

Maryland
Johns Hopkins University
School of Medicine
Baltimore 21218

University of Maryland School
of Medicine
Baltimore 21201

Massachusetts
Boston University School of
Medicine
Boston 02215

Harvard Medical School
Boston 02138

Tufts University School of
Medicine
Boston 02155

University of Massachusetts
School of Medicine
Worcester 01605

Michigan
Michigan State University
College of Human Medicine
East Lansing 48823

University of Michigan Medical
School
Ann Arbor 48104

Wayne State University
School of Medicine
Detroit 48202

Minnesota
The Mayo Medical School
Rochester 55901

University of Minnesota at
Duluth Medical Education
Program
Duluth 55812

University of Minnesota
Medical School
Minneapolis 55455

Mississippi
University of Mississippi
School of Medicine
Jackson 39216

Missouri
St. Louis University School
of Medicine
St. Louis 63103

University of Missouri School
of Medicine
Columbia 65201

University of Missouri School
of Medicine
Kansas City 64110

Washington University School
of Medicine
St. Louis 63130

Nebraska
Creighton University School
of Medicine
Omaha 68178

University of Nebraska
College of Medicine
Omaha 68105

Nevada
University of Nevada School
of Medicine
Reno 89507

New Hampshire
Dartmouth Medical School
Hanover 03755

New Jersey
College of Medicine and
Dentistry of New Jersey
New Jersey Medical School
Newark 07103

College of Medicine and
Dentistry of New Jersey
Rutgers Medical School
New Brunswick 08903

New Mexico
University of New Mexico
School of Medicine
Albuquerque 87131

New York
Albany Medical College of
Union University
Albany 12208

Albert Einstein College of
Medicine of Yeshiva
University
New York (Bronx) 10033

Columbia University College
of Physicians and Surgeons
New York 10027

Cornell University Medical
College
New York 10021

Mount Sinai School of
Medicine
New York 10029

New York Medical College
Flower and Fifth Avenue
Hospitals
New York 10029

New York University School
of Medicine
New York 10016

State University of New York
at Buffalo School of
Medicine
Buffalo 14214

State University of New York
Downstate Medical Center
College of Medicine
New York (Brooklyn) 11203

State University of New York
(Stony Brook) Health
Sciences Center
Stony Brook 11790

State University of New York
Upstate Medical Center
College of Medicine
Syracuse 13210

University of Rochester School
of Medicine and Dentistry
Rochester 14627

North Carolina
Bowman Gray School of
Medicine of Wake Forest
University
Winston-Salem 27109

Duke University School of
Medicine
Durham 27706

East Carolina University
Division of Medical Sciences
Greenville 27834

University of North Carolina
School of Medicine
Chapel Hill 27514

North Dakota
University of North Dakota
School of Medicine
Grand Forks 58201

Ohio
Case-Western Reserve
University School of Medicine
Cleveland 44106

Medical College of Ohio at
Toledo
Toledo 43614

Ohio State University College
of Medicine
Columbus 43210

University of Cincinnati
College of Medicine
Cincinnati 45221

Wright State University School
of Medicine
Dayton 45431

Oklahoma
University of Oklahoma School
of Medicine
Oklahoma City 73190

Oregon
University of Oregon Medical
School
Portland 97201

Pennsylvania
Hahnemann Medical College
Philadelphia 19102

Jefferson Medical College of
Thomas Jefferson University
Philadelphia 19107

Medical College of
Pennsylvania
Philadelphia 19129

Pennsylvania State University
College of Medicine
Milton S. Hershey Medical
Center
Hershey 17033

Temple University School of
Medicine
Philadelphia 19122

University of Pennsylvania
School of Medicine
Philadelphia 19174

University of Pittsburgh
Pittsburgh 15260

Rhode Island
Brown University Program in
Medical Science
Providence 02912

South Carolina
Medical University of South
Carolina
Charleston 29401

University of South Carolina
School of Medicine
Columbia 29208

South Dakota
University of South Dakota
School of Medicine
Vermillion 57069

Tennessee
Meharry Medical College
School of Medicine
Nashville 37208

University of Tennesse
College of Medicine
Memphis 38163

Vanderbilt University School
of Medicine
Nashville 37240

Texas
Baylor University College of
Medicine
Houston 77025

Texas Technological University
School of Medicine
Lubbock 79409

University of Texas Medical
  School
Galveston 77550

University of Texas Medical
  School
Houston 77025

University of Texas Medical
  School
San Antonio 78284

University of Texas
  Southwestern Medical
  School
Dallas 75235

Utah
  University of Utah College
    of Medicine
  Salt Lake City 84112

Vermont
  University of Vermont College
    of Medicine
  Burlington 05401

Virginia
  Eastern Virginia Medical
    School
  Norfolk 23507

Medical College of Virginia
  School of Medicine
Richmond 23284

University of Virginia School
  of Medicine
Charlottesville 22903

Washington
  University of Washington
    School of Medicine
  Seattle 98195

West Virginia
  West Virginia University
    School of Medicine
  Morgantown 26506

Wisconsin
  Medical College of Wisconsin
  Milwaukee 53233

University of Wisconsin
  Medical School
  Madison 53706

INDEX

Accreditation, professional, 105-109; American Board of Psychiatry and Neurology, 108; American Psychiatric Association (APA), 107-108; certification, 106; licensing, 105-106; professional organizations, 106-107

American Board of Psychiatry and Neurology, Inc., 106, 108

American Medical College Application Service (AMCAS), 54, 55

American Psychiatric Association (APA), 22, 29, 30, 58, 61, 62, 85, 93, 94, 96, 103, 106, 107-108, 111, 114, 117, 118, 119

Aristotle, 15

Beers, Clifford, 17

Chapman, A. H., 47

College, 50-53; costs, 63-70; curricula, 52-53; financial aid, 71-76

A Descriptive Directory of Psychiatric Training Programs in the U.S., 1972-73 (APA), 61, 103

Directory of Approved Internships and Residencies (AMA), 61

Dix, Dorothea Lynde, 17

Education, for psychiatry, 49-76; college, 50-53; costs (college and medical school), 63   ; financial aid, 71-76; high school, 49-50; internship, 60-61; medical schools (American), 53-57; medical schools (foreign), 57-58; medical schools (large vs. small), 58-60; medical schools (list of), 136-141

Employment, 93-104; future outlook, 100; geographic distribution, 94-95; places of, 93-97; salaries, 101-104; in special communities, 98; types of, 93-94; urban versus rural, 97-98

Financial aid, college and medical school, 71-76; cooperative programs, 73; grants, 74-75; loans, 75-76; other sources, 76; scholarships, 73-74

Franklin, Benjamin, 16-17

Freud, Sigmund, 17

Getting started, 77-92; interviews, 90-92; resumes, 87-88

Guide for Residency Programs in Psychiatry and Neurology, 61-62

High school preparation, 49-50

Hippocrates, 15

Internship, medical school, 60-61

Interviews, job, 90-92

It's All Arranged, 15 Hours in a Psychiatrist's Life, 47

Joint Commission on Mental Health of Children, 22

Lowry, Fern, 34

Medical College Admission Assessment Program (MCAAP), 56

Medical College Admission Test (MCAT), 56

Medical schools, American, 53-57; costs, 63-70; financial aid, 71-76; foreign, 57-58; large vs. small, 58-60; list of, 136-141; internship, 60-61; residency, 60-63

Mental Health Directory, 85

Mental illness, 21-30; definition of, 21-23; treatment of, 30; types of, 23-25

[Min]ority groups, financial aid for, 115-117; opportunities for, 111-117; special programs for, 112-115

[N]ational Board of Medical Examiners, 105

[N]ational Committee for Mental Hygiene, 18

National Institute of Mental Health (NIMH), 98, 99, 100, 124

Neurology, 45

Pennsylvania Hospital (Philadelphia), 17

Personality disorders, 25

Plato, 15

Psychiatric News, 85

Psychiatrists, and allied specialists, 44-48; as citizens, 42-44; as human beings, 32-35; as professionals, 35-42; definition of, 31-32

Psychiatry, definition of, 11; education for, 49-76; employment and salaries for, 93-104; and ethics, 109; future of, 123-129; getting started in, 77-92; and mental illness, 21-30; and professional accreditation, 105-109; women and minority groups in, 111-121

Psychoanalysis, 44-45

Psychology, clinical, 45

Psychoneuroses, 23-24

Psychoses, 24-25

Related fields, 44-48

Residency, medical school, 60-63; salaries, 103-104

Resumes, 87-88

Rush, Benjamin, 16-17

Salaries, 101-103

Social work, psychiatric, 45

A Survey of Academic Rese[arch] in Psychiatric Residenc[y] Training, 62

Therapy, 26-27; behavior[al modifi]cation, 29; chemother[apy or] drug, 28; family, 28; [group,] 28; hypnosis (hypno[sis),] 27; psychodrama (r[ole-playing),] 28; shock, 28-29

Women, opportunities

University of Texas Medical School
Galveston 77550

University of Texas Medical School
Houston 77025

University of Texas Medical School
San Antonio 78284

University of Texas Southwestern Medical School
Dallas 75235

Utah
University of Utah College of Medicine
Salt Lake City 84112

Vermont
University of Vermont College of Medicine
Burlington 05401

Virginia
Eastern Virginia Medical School
Norfolk 23507

Medical College of Virginia School of Medicine
Richmond 23284

University of Virginia School of Medicine
Charlottesville 22903

Washington
University of Washington School of Medicine
Seattle 98195

West Virginia
West Virginia University School of Medicine
Morgantown 26506

Wisconsin
Medical College of Wisconsin
Milwaukee 53233

University of Wisconsin Medical School
Madison 53706

INDEX

Accreditation, professional, 105-
109; American Board of
Psychiatry and Neurology,
108; American Psychiatric
Association (APA), 107-108;
certification, 106; licensing,
105-106; professional organizations, 106-107

American Board of Psychiatry
and Neurology, Inc., 106, 108

American Medical College Application Service (AMCAS), 54, 55

American Psychiatric Association
(APA), 22, 29, 30, 58, 61, 62,
85, 93, 94, 96, 103, 106, 107-
108, 111, 114, 117, 118, 119

Aristotle, 15

Beers, Clifford, 17

Chapman, A. H., 47

College, 50-53; costs, 63-70;
curricula, 52-53; financial
aid, 71-76

*A Descriptive Directory of
Psychiatric Training Programs
in the U.S., 1972-73* (APA),
61, 103

*Directory of Approved Intern-
ships and Residencies* (AMA),
61

Dix, Dorothea Lynde, 17

Education, for psychiatry, 49-76;
college, 50-53; costs (college

and medical school), 63 ';
financial aid, 71-76; higi
school, 49-50; internshi
60-61; medical schools
(American), 53-57; medical
schools (foreign), 57-58;
medical schools (large vs.
small), 58-60; medical
schools (list of), 136-141

Employment, 93-104; future
outlook, 100; geographic
distribution, 94-95; places of,
93-97; salaries, 101-104; in
special communities, 98;
types of, 93-94; urban versus
rural, 97-98

Financial aid, college and medical
school, 71-76; cooperative
programs, 73; grants, 74-75;
loans, 75-76; other sources,
76; scholarships, 73-74

Franklin, Benjamin, 16-17

Freud, Sigmund, 17

Getting started, 77-92; interviews,
90-92; resumes, 87-88

*Guide for Residency Programs in
Psychiatry and Neurology,*
61-62

High school preparation, 49-50

Hippocrates, 15

Internship, medical school, 60-61

Interviews, job, 90-92

It's All Arranged, 15 Hours in a Psychiatrist's Life, 47

Joint Commission on Mental Health of Children, 22

Lowry, Fern, 34

Medical College Admission Assessment Program (MCAAP), 56

Medical College Admission Test (MCAT), 56

Medical schools, American, 53-57; costs, 63-70; financial aid, 71-76; foreign, 57-58; large vs. small, 58-60; list of, 136-141; internship, 60-61; residency, 60-63

Mental Health Directory, 85

Mental illness, 21-30; definition of, 21-23; treatment of, 30; types of, 23-25

minority groups, financial aid for, 115-117; opportunities for, 111-117; special programs for, 112-115

National Board of Medical Examiners, 105

National Committee for Mental Hygiene, 18

National Institute of Mental Health (NIMH), 98, 99, 100, 124

Neurology, 45

Pennsylvania Hospital (Philadelphia), 17

Personality disorders, 25

Plato, 15

Psychiatric News, 85

Psychiatrists, and allied specialists, 44-48; as citizens, 42-44; as human beings, 32-35; as professionals, 35-42; definition of, 31-32

Psychiatry, definition of, 11; education for, 49-76; employment and salaries for, 93-104; and ethics, 109; future of, 123-129; getting started in, 77-92; and mental illness, 21-30; and professional accreditation, 105-109; women and minority groups in, 111-121

Psychoanalysis, 44-45

Psychology, clinical, 45

Psychoneuroses, 23-24

Psychoses, 24-25

Related fields, 44-48

Residency, medical school, 60-63; salaries, 103-104

Resumes, 87-88

Rush, Benjamin, 16-17

Salaries, 101-103

Social work, psychiatric, 45

A Survey of Academic Resources in Psychiatric Residency Training, 62

Therapy, 26-27; behavior modification, 29; chemotherapy, 29; drug, 28; family, 28; gestalt, 28; hypnosis (hypnotherapy), 27; psychodrama (role-playing), 28; shock, 28-29

Women, opportunities for, 117-121